Cambridge Elements

Elements in Evolutionary Economics
edited by
John Foster
University of Queensland
Jason Potts
RMIT University
Isabel Almudi
University of Zaragoza
Francisco Fatas-Villafranca
University of Zaragoza
David A. Harper
New York University

ENTREPRENEURSHIP AND EVOLUTIONARY ECONOMICS

Per L. Bylund
Oklahoma State University

Shaftesbury Road, Cambridge CB2 8EA, United Kingdom

One Liberty Plaza, 20th Floor, New York, NY 10006, USA

477 Williamstown Road, Port Melbourne, VIC 3207, Australia

314–321, 3rd Floor, Plot 3, Splendor Forum, Jasola District Centre, New Delhi – 110025, India

103 Penang Road, #05-06/07, Visioncrest Commercial, Singapore 238467

Cambridge University Press is part of Cambridge University Press & Assessment, a department of the University of Cambridge.

We share the University's mission to contribute to society through the pursuit of education, learning and research at the highest international levels of excellence.

www.cambridge.org
Information on this title: www.cambridge.org/9781009540223

DOI: 10.1017/9781009540186

© Per L. Bylund 2025

This publication is in copyright. Subject to statutory exception and to the provisions of relevant collective licensing agreements, no reproduction of any part may take place without the written permission of Cambridge University Press & Assessment.

When citing this work, please include a reference to the DOI 10.1017/9781009540186

First published 2025

A catalogue record for this publication is available from the British Library

ISBN 978-1-009-54022-3 Hardback
ISBN 978-1-009-54019-3 Paperback
ISSN 2514-3573 (online)
ISSN 2514-3581 (print)

Cambridge University Press & Assessment has no responsibility for the persistence or accuracy of URLs for external or third-party internet websites referred to in this publication and does not guarantee that any content on such websites is, or will remain, accurate or appropriate.

Entrepreneurship and Evolutionary Economics

Elements in Evolutionary Economics

DOI: 10.1017/9781009540186
First published online: March 2025

Per L. Bylund
Oklahoma State University

Author for correspondence: Per L. Bylund, Per.Bylund@okstate.edu

Abstract: Entrepreneurship has been expunged from contemporary mainstream economics despite being an important driver and cause of economic development and growth. However, whereas Evolutionary Economics recognizes value-creative entrepreneurship, its role and impact tend to still be understated and the vast implications not fully understood. This Element attempts to remedy this by theorizing on how entrepreneurship impacts and drives market economies, the implications for economic change and renewal, and how the pursuit of new value creation determines the evolution of an economy. We find that allowing for entrepreneurial new value creation – innovative entrepreneurship – produces a different and more dynamic understanding of the market as a process, the role of knowledge and uncertainty, economic evolution and progress, as well as has important implications for political economy.

Keywords: entrepreneurship, innovation, value creation, market process, economic growth

© Per L. Bylund 2025

ISBNs: 9781009540223 (HB), 9781009540193 (PB), 9781009540186 (OC)
ISSNs: 2514-3573 (online), 2514-3581 (print)

Contents

1 Economics: Evolutionary and Entrepreneurial   1

2 Scopes of Entrepreneurship   9

3 The Entrepreneurial Market Process   20

4 Political Economy   40

5 Concluding Remarks   51

   References   53

1 Economics: Evolutionary and Entrepreneurial

Modern economics is surprisingly static considering the object of its study. Economic models and explanations tend to be based on the assumption that markets are in equilibrium and that they will quickly reestablish equilibrium should economic data change. Simply put, as it is currently exercised, economics lacks support for dynamism. It cannot explain how economies evolve, unfold, and progress over time.

This is a rather recent development, however, and not representative of the study of economics *in toto*. Indeed, dynamism is core to economics traditions outside of the contemporary mainstream as well as in earlier theorizing. It was only when economics turned to formal modeling in the 20th century (Blaug 2003) that it turned to static analysis and, importantly, abandoned entrepreneurship as the endogenous cause and driver of change. Modern economic models tend to exclude the phenomenon of entrepreneurship altogether and with it economic dynamism.

After all, there can be no entrepreneurship in general equilibrium because the economy is already assumed to be in its maximizing state (e.g., Jones 1965). And under so-called perfect competition – "an economy with complete knowledge" (Stigler 1957, 11) – there is similarly no space for the entrepreneur because opportunities are known by all and economic profits are therefore zero. Not to mention that entrepreneurship is elusive and difficult to specify. As the source of novelty, and thus cause of disruption and the evolutionary progression of an economy, entrepreneurship may even undermine the assumptions that facilitate formal modeling and precise predictions. Therefore, by assumption, the models have neither entrepreneurs nor endogenous causes of novelty, which allows the economist to calculate maximizing behaviors and therefore estimate "optimality." Models, as Milton Friedman (1953) famously argued, may benefit from unrealistic or even alien assumptions if they can still predict economic outcomes. This has led to an economics in which the entrepreneur is no longer recognized as a core player in the economy, but has instead become "the specter who haunts our economic models" (Baumol 1993, 197).

Entrepreneurship, and with it the engine of economic change, has been "expunged" from modern mainstream economics (Baumol 1968, 66). The earlier understanding of the economy as a "process of industrial mutation" (Schumpeter 1947, 85), an *evolutionary* process undergoing constant renewal, was abandoned to make modeling practicable.

1.1 Evolutionary Economics

Modern mainstream economics is not without critics, including from within the academic economics profession. One such critique takes the evolutionary nature of an economy to heart. It was originally formulated by Richard R. Nelson and Sidney G. Winter (1973, 1982), who presented an alternative approach to explaining economic growth based on what they referred to as the "Schumpeterian alternative" (Nelson and Winter 1974; cf. Schumpeter 1934). This approach is based on two premises: that "economic change is important and interesting" and that "a major reconstruction of the theoretical foundations of our discipline is a precondition for significant growth in our understanding of economic change" (Nelson and Winter 1982, 3–4).

Nelson and Winter's work spawned a "new wave" of approaches to economic theorizing under the umbrella term *Evolutionary Economics* (Hodgson 2019). These approaches have in common that they recognize the economy as an evolving, evolutionary system in which productive capabilities are subject to a Darwinian process of variation-selection-replication. As Potts and Dopfer (2024, 20) put it, "an economy [is] made of habits and routines, capabilities and technologies, from which entrepreneurial action generates variation, market processes generate selection, and knowledge is replicated in firms, etc." The evolutionary process is thus instigated by entrepreneurs who introduce variation in the form of new technology (e.g., Metcalfe 2002; Nelson 2005) that is intended to produce new and valuable production capabilities. Technology, writes Dopfer (2005, 53), "is conceived of as an instrument for serving economic purposes" that "is mostly used in a productive context to perform complex productive tasks."

As successful (proven) new technology is replicated and therefore propagates through the economy, the economy, and specifically economic growth, is a process of generating and accumulating *knowledge* (Malerba and McKelvey 2019, 2020; Koppl et al. 2023) of productive capabilities. However, as we will argue in Section 3.1, this presumes the economics of technological development, which is a matter of value-motivated innovation – novel production undertaken in the pursuit of creating new value. In other words, it is a matter of entrepreneurship.

1.2 Entrepreneurship: Origin and Meaning

Entrepreneurship has been identified as the "driving force of the market, the element tending toward unceasing innovation and improvement" (Mises 1998, 256) – the entrepreneur is the innovator, a creator of novelty and new value (Schumpeter 1934). Thus, an economy without entrepreneurship is not only a simplified and perhaps bland model of the buzzling and vibrant real-world market but a fundamentally and altogether different construct (Bylund 2022a, 2024).

Israel M. Kirzner (1997, 39; emphases in original) puts it thus:

> In order to perceive regularities amidst the apparently chaotic vagaries of real-world market volatility, it may seem methodologically sound to imagine a world with *no* scope for entrepreneurship. Yet, paradoxically, exactly the opposite is the case. It is *only* when entrepreneurship is introduced that we begin to appreciate how and why markets work.

The study of entrepreneurship is at least as old as the study of economics (Thornton 1998). Indeed, entrepreneurship had a pivotal role (Brown and Thornton 2013) already in Richard Cantillon's *Essai Sur La Nature Du Commerce En Général* published in 1755 (Hébert and Link 2009), often regarded the very first economics treatise (Jevons 1905).

To Cantillon (1931), what characterizes entrepreneurship is economic action for which the costs are known but the revenues are not. In other words, Cantillon defines the entrepreneur as an *uncertainty-bearer* who takes resources at given prices, transforms them through some productive activity, and then presents the results to potential buyers with hopes that they will purchase them at a selling price higher than their already incurred cost. The bearing of uncertainty, or the risk of suffering losses in pursuit of unknown profits, remains a core aspect of our understanding of entrepreneurship today (e.g., McMullen and Shepherd 2006; McKelvie, Haynie, and Gustavsson 2011).

What is curious about Cantillon's discussion is not how he uses the term, which from the perspective of today's entrepreneurship scholarship appears rather standard, but how he *changed* it. Cantillon in fact turned the meaning on its head (Thornton 2020; cf. Hébert and Link 2009, 5). The word "entrepreneur"[1] had previously referred specifically to government contractors, who were generally regarded as unreliable cheaters because they produced for the government at fixed prices and therefore could only (and did) maximize their profits by reducing costs. They often did so by compromising on quality and cutting corners in other ways.

Cantillon chose to use the term "entrepreneurship" differently: known costs but unknown revenues (and thus profits). That Cantillon was able to pull off the feat of changing (if not reversing) the definition of entrepreneurship is indicative of his treatise's great influence on the bourgeoning field of economics. Not only does Adam Smith, generally recognized as the "father" of economics, repeatedly cite Cantillon in his *An Inquiry into the Nature and Causes of the Wealth of Nations* published in 1776 (Smith 1976) but Mark Thornton (2020) notes that many influential thinkers in economics broadly were directly

---

[1] Translations of Cantillon's *Essai* (e.g., 1931) have used the term "undertaker," but Cantillon used "entrepreneur" in the original French.

influenced by Cantillon's work: from François Quesnay and the Physiocrats to A. R. J. Turgot and J. B. Say.

Playing such a central role in Cantillon's *Essai*, entrepreneurship theory arguably "created" economics (Thornton 1998; Brown and Thornton 2013).

1.3 Entrepreneurship: Evolution and Use

Entrepreneurship has played a fundamental and important role in economic theorizing since Cantillon. During this time, it has taken on different meanings and uses. Its precise implications have varied between economists and schools of economic thought as different theories and theorists have leveraged the entrepreneurship function to explain a range of phenomena and processes.

In their historical overview of the uses of entrepreneurship in the history of economic thought, Robert F. Hébert and Albert N. Link (2009, 100–101; cf. 1988) identify twelve distinct but overlapping roles:

1. The entrepreneur is the person who assumes the risk associated with uncertainty (Cantillon, von Thünen, von Mangoldt, Mill, Hawley, Knight, von Mises, Cole, Shackle).
2. The entrepreneur is the person who supplies financial capital (Smith, Turgot, von Böhm-Bawerk, Edgeworth, Pigou, von Mises).
3. The entrepreneur is an innovator (Baudeau, Bentham, von Thünen, Schmoller, Sombart, Weber, Schumpeter).
4. The entrepreneur is a decision-maker (Cantillon, Menger, Marshall, von Wieser, Amasa Walker, Francis Walker, Keynes, von Mises, Shackle, Cole, Schultz).
5. The entrepreneur is an industrial leader (Say, Saint-Simon, Amasa Walker, Francis Walker, Marshall, von Wieser, Sombart, Weber, Schumpeter).
6. The entrepreneur is a manager or superintendent (Say, Mill, Marshall, Menger).
7. The entrepreneur is an organizer and coordinator of economic resources (Say, Walras, von Wieser, Schmoller, Sombart, Weber, Clark, Davenport, Schumpeter, Coase).
8. The entrepreneur is the owner of an enterprise (Quesnay, von Wieser, Pigou, Hawley).
9. The entrepreneur is an employer of factors of production (e.g., Amasa Walker, Francis Walker, von Wieser, Keynes).
10. The entrepreneur is a contractor (Bentham).
11. The entrepreneur is an arbitrageur (Cantillon, Walras, Kirzner).
12. The entrepreneur is an allocator of resources among alternative uses (Cantillon, Kirzner, Schultz).

The list of theoretical applications is illuminating for several reasons. First, it shows the pervasiveness of entrepreneurship in economic theorizing. The scholars listed are among the thinkers in economics and beyond who created and shaped the field and made it into the highly influential body of theory that we know today. Second, although the meaning of entrepreneurship varies, the different uses revolve around active change in and to the economy: the entrepreneur is involved in, if not the cause of, most or all of the change processes in the market. The role of the entrepreneur is therefore closely related to or the driver of economic value creation – and therefore central to how and why economies evolve over time.

1.4 The Economic Function

Importantly, the entrepreneur in economic theory is not the person, such as the founder of a business or a businessman but refers to the *function* provided in the economy. Economics is traditionally the study of functions and how they relate to, if not *cause* (cf. Menger 2007), observable economic phenomena. Whereas most economists are methodologically individualist (Schumpeter 1909), meaning they find that agency and valuation rest ultimately with individuals rather than collectives or groups of individuals, economics is not the study of the individual per se. After all, we are complex beings who act in different ways with different purposes and implications: a single person can be both a producer and a consumer as well as laborer, capitalist, and entrepreneur.

For economic analysis, it matters not what person is carrying out labor or entrepreneurship but the implications of the function, the role it plays in the economic system. It is based on this function that we can explain its compensation (if any), which economists have long attempted to understand. This is also part of the price system and therefore the bottom-up allocation of resources between production processes in an economy (Hayek 1945). Whereas factors of production, such as land and labor, earn economic rents as determined by their respective market prices (rent, wages), entrepreneurship has generally been understood as earning *profit* (e.g., Knight 1921) from bearing the uncertainty of productive enterprise.

Mises well put it:

> The specific entrepreneurial function consists in determining the employment of the factors of production. The entrepreneur is the man who dedicates them to special purposes. In doing so he is driven solely by the selfish interest in making profits and in acquiring wealth. But he cannot evade the law of the market. He can succeed only by best serving the consumers. His profit depends on the approval of his conduct by the consumers. (Mises 1998, 288)

The role of the entrepreneur is to find and realize new and better ways to create value understood as consumer want satisfaction facilitated by the production of goods and services.[2] The entrepreneur, thus, causes change to the economy's production structure (e.g., Bylund 2015d) by, for example, "the carrying out of new combinations" of factors (Schumpeter 1934, 66).

The entrepreneur may suffer a loss (earn a profit) if costs exceed revenues (revenues exceed costs), but *the person* who is that entrepreneur can still have been fully compensated for his contribution of labor and management services as well as land (such as office space) to the enterprise. In other words, the person John Smith who has started a business may have more money at the end of a year than at the beginning despite suffering a loss *as entrepreneur*. This is not splitting hairs as we are not, as economists, interested in the person John Smith or his financial status – and also not whether or to what extent he acts as laborer, manager, landowner, or entrepreneur. We are interested in the economics of *the functions*. The impact of entrepreneurship in the economy is distinct from the impact of labor or land ownership, and what matters to understanding the economy is the implications of entrepreneurship compared to implications of other, logically separable functions.

Despite not theorizing on the function of entrepreneurship, contemporary economics recognizes that entrepreneurship has important implications for economic growth and thus for policy. In other words, economists must account for the observable implications of entrepreneurship in the real economy. This has generated a mass of research, predominantly empirical and relating to public policy (e.g., Wennekers and Thurik 1999; Carree and Thurik 2010), that deals with entrepreneurship but deviates from the traditional study of the function within and with respect to the evolution of an economy.

Peter G. Klein (2008) usefully distinguishes between three different perspectives on entrepreneurship in the literature: occupational, structural, and functional. They each have different units of analysis and define entrepreneurship in different ways. Occupational research focuses on the individual and sees entrepreneurship as the choice to be self-employed over employed by others (e.g., Lazear 2004; Parker 2004; Levine and Rubinstein 2017). Structural research instead focuses on the firm or industry and defines as entrepreneurial the small

---

[2] Value is the satisfaction that a good or service provides a consumer when using that good or service. It is subjective and immeasurable and exists only in the reduction or removal of some felt uneasiness. The expectation of such value thus determines the consumer's willingness to pay for a good or service offered for sale. The consumer's opportunity cost is the anticipated value of other known or expected uses for their purchasing power. Ultimately, a good's market price approximates (in money terms) the satisfaction it brings consumers compared to other goods.

firm such that an industry is entrepreneurial if it consists of many small, as opposed to a few large, firms (e.g., Brock and Evans 1989; Acs 1992).

In contrast to occupational and structural research, Klein notes that the classical contributions to entrepreneurship theory in economics "model entrepreneurship as a *function*, activity, or process, not an employment category or market structure" (Klein 2008, 177, emphasis in original). This is what we will do in this Element as well, which allows us to theorize on *how* the economy evolves and at the same time avoid the explanatory limitations of the other approaches. To explain the evolution of the economy in terms of entrepreneurship, it is not sufficient to treat it as merely occupational choice or market structure, although they may be important too. We need to look at the distinct function of entrepreneurship, its scope and implications.

1.5 Entrepreneurship in Evolutionary Economics

In Evolutionary Economics, the entrepreneurship function is understood in the Schumpeterian sense of causing economic change: "Schumpeter pointed out the right problem – how to understand economic change – and his vision encompassed many of the important elements of the answer" (Nelson and Winter 1982, ix). Simply put, entrepreneurship is in Evolutionary Economics understood as *innovation* (Schumpeter 1934)[3] – "a central characteristic of modern capitalist economies" (Nelson 2018, 3) – and the "entrepreneur is the leader who leads the firm to new [production] techniques" (Winter 2006, 136).

Whereas the entrepreneur introduces new technology, the manager of a firm deals with the already existing "routine" knowledge and supervises operation of production techniques that are well-known: "organizations are based in their internal interactions on behavioral routines, rules of thumb and regular interaction patterns" (Witt 1994, 543). Within the circular flow of an equilibrium economy (cf. Schumpeter 1934), all possibilities within the production set are known and the manager thus maximizes profit by positioning the firm with respect to exogenously determined market prices and technological conditions (Winter 2006). This knowledge therefore drives and, ultimately, determines firm behavior.

When the knowledge changes, or new knowledge is introduced, firms consequently change their behavior. Successful innovations, which make information of new productive technology available to the market, push out the production possibilities frontier. This forces existing firms to adapt to the new technologies – the new data – or risk being left behind or become obsolete. In this sense, entrepreneurship acts on the unknown and conquers it to create, diffuse, and

---

[3] We will discuss Schumpeter's work in greater detail in Section 3.3.

use new production knowledge (Malerba and McKelvey 2019, 2020). The entrepreneurial creation of new production technology introduces variation in the economy, which is then subjected to market selection pressure and then, where successful, replicated (Nelson and Winter 1982, 266–72).

As economic changes wrought by entrepreneurs have no obvious end point but may give rise to several possible new equilibria, economists must analyze "'out of equilibrium' behavior" (Nelson 1995, 52) to determine which equilibrium is more likely to be attained. The evolutionary approach therefore shifts our attention from maximizing resource allocation in static equilibrium to the evolutionary *processes* of economic change: the "questions are . . . why and how knowledge, preferences, technology, and institutions change in the historical process, and what impact these changes have on the state of the economy at any point in time" (Witt 2006, 2).

The entrepreneur plays a major role in economic change by introducing new knowledge, which in turn causes shifts in firm behavior and therefore economic change. To Schumpeter, innovations – "new combinations" – are typically introduced through new firms rather than old ones: "in general it is not the owner of stage-coaches who builds railways," as he put it (Schumpeter 1934, 66). But old firms can also act entrepreneurially by adopting innovative behavior or investing in new technologies, which when implemented often has effects on the organization, its routines and output, beyond what can be predicted (Winter 2006).

Whether in new or old firms, the opportunity for profit that the entrepreneur discovers is not itself created but implied in the economic system (Buenstorf 2007). The same is true for the knowledge that entrepreneurs generate, which is readily discoverable through innovative action – trial and error – but perhaps not fully predictable before the fact. The entrepreneur in Evolutionary Economics is thus a discoverer of what is already implied but not yet or not fully discovered, a catalyst for economic change but not an ultimate cause that creates change *ex nihili*. The evolutionary approach is focused on "the interactions between innovation, technology institutions, and economic dynamics" (Malerba and McKelvey 2020, 505).

What we will argue in this Element is that Evolutionary Economics adopts a too narrow perspective of entrepreneurship. It does not take into account the imagination of the entrepreneur, which can be informed and inspired by what is but not therefore limited by it, and the value of what is created as *determined by consumers after the fact*. As we will see, entrepreneurship is better understood as imaginative value creation than the discovery or generation of new knowledge. In fact, by recognizing the uncertainty implied in market-based innovation, the economy cannot be understood in terms of knowledge and the market process – and, indeed, economic growth – is not the accumulation of knowledge.

2 Scopes of Entrepreneurship

To understand the role and impact of entrepreneurship, it is helpful to use a conceptual model of the economy in which we can introduce increasing degrees of dynamics and change and, as a result, trace how (and if) the role, scope, and impact of entrepreneurship changes. Thus, we can explore the theoretical limits of entrepreneurship as a market function. While doing so, we can also define this function and shed light on its implications for the structure and evolution of the economy.

Our basic assumption here is that the role of the entrepreneur is to bear the uncertainty of economic value production. In essence, the entrepreneur dedicates productive resources to specific production processes in anticipation of potential gains from increased value output. Profits are therefore earned from finding and realizing resources' greater value-production. Value here refers to the satisfaction that produced goods are expected to provide consumers at the time they purchase the produced consumer goods (Menger 2007). In other words, (expected) higher-valued goods command higher market prices that, in turn, represent the greater value contribution of the resources used in their production (we will return to this in Section 3.5).

Ours is a theoretical exploration of the meaning as well as the scope and implications of entrepreneurship. The expected outcome of this exercise is to explain the economic process as determined by the entrepreneurship function – the scopes of economic evolution as brought about by entrepreneurship. By doing this step by step – relaxing the assumptions of the model in order to allow for increasing entrepreneurial scope – we can identify types of entrepreneurial functions and their respective impact. This, in turn, provides a means for categorizing existing (and new) theories of entrepreneurship. It should also provide insight into how and to what extent entrepreneurship can generate or effectuate economic development and growth. Doing this will also shed light on the limitations of entrepreneurship as the function is conceptualized in Evolutionary Economics.

We will look at three simple models of the market economy with different and increasing scope for entrepreneurship. In the first and simplest model, we assume that the economy is not already in a maximizing state. Resources may therefore be imperfectly allocated, and it may be possible to find better (more value-creative) uses for them. No one has perfect foresight, but circumstances do not meaningfully change. The role of the entrepreneur is here to figure out how to improve the allocation of productive resources and thereby earn profit.

In the second model, we add complexity by allowing circumstances to change. Production can here be affected by exogenous shocks and other changes, including changing consumer preferences. This means entrepreneurs must, in addition to finding better resource allocations (as in the first model), both respond to and attempt to meet expected (or imagined) changes to improve the market's value output.

The third model, which is the most dynamic and complex, adds the possibility of changes to the market "from within." Specifically, we look at the impact of endogenously generated changes that are created, enacted, or attempted by the disruptive entrepreneur.

2.1 Model 1: Resource Allocation

In this simplest of our models, the economy is not currently in general equilibrium. There are thus inefficiencies in its production apparatus, which means resources have been put to nonmaximizing (but still productive) uses. In other words, whereas resources are already used in production, they are underutilized in value terms. This translates to an opportunity for gain if and to the extent that these resources are reallocated to where they contribute to greater value output.

Model 1 constitutes a very simple form of disequilibrium limited to inefficient resource allocations. We hold other parameters such as resource supply, technological knowledge, and consumer preferences constant. There are no changes, exogenous or endogenous, to impact the economy other than attempts to reallocate resources toward greater value output. Thus, any gains from improving the overall resource allocation are permanent. This means the economy has a stable efficient end-state that is potentially reachable by exhausting all opportunities for more value-productive resource allocation.

An implication of this is that all resources with known productive uses should already be used in production. No new knowledge will be generated other than what is learned by reallocating resources to generate greater value output. As a result, there should be no idle productive resources because those would constitute an unnecessary and avoidable loss for the resource owner.

This model is of course highly unrealistic, but the point is to separate out the effect of entrepreneurship as a strictly allocative function. (We will add complexity in Models 2 and 3.) Entrepreneurs are here, in Model 1, in the business only of reallocating resources toward what they anticipate will be more valuable uses, from which they will earn higher returns.

Model 1 already provides several important insights. First, disequilibrium is a prerequisite for entrepreneurship. Because the economy is not in equilibrium there are differences in returns to productive resources and thus opportunities for entrepreneurs to reallocate them in hopes of earning greater returns. Were there no differences and thus no opportunities for gain, there would be no entrepreneurship. (This indirectly also offers support for our claim above that equilibrium models lack entrepreneurship.)

Second, by reallocating a resource from production process A to production process B, whether or not the change successfully increases value output, the quantities of the resource used in *both* processes change. As process A now uses less of that resource, the value returns per unit should increase per the law of diminishing marginal utility: the lower quantity of the produced good therefore commands a higher market price. Similarly, as there is more of the resource in process B, the value returns per unit should there decrease. The higher/lower market prices for the produced goods means the value contributions (and thus prices) of resources used in the respective processes change accordingly. It follows that reallocation of resources is a type of arbitrage between returns in different productive uses (Kirzner 1973). It also follows that reallocating one resource may in turn uncover that other resources are also misallocated.

Third, as entrepreneurs do not have perfect foresight, as is generally the case in equilibrium models or what Kirzner (1973) calls "Robbinsian maximizing," they cannot be expected to always improve resource allocation but can also, despite trying to do otherwise, cause misallocations. The obvious case is if an entrepreneur overshoots and so reallocates too much of a resource from a production process A to production process B. This causes a new misallocation as the resource is now overallocated to production process B rather than, as was previously the case, production process A.

We cannot, of course, assume that there is only a single entrepreneur in the market or that only one entrepreneur notices (or imagines) discrepancies in returns to a resource between production processes. We also do not assume that allocating productive resources from and to production processes is instantaneous – some time must pass before the resources are put into use in their new allocations. It can be the case, therefore, that several entrepreneurs discover that a resource is misallocated and simultaneously act to reallocate this resource, thereby causing the resource to be underallocated where it was previously overallocated. In other words, entrepreneurs' combined reallocation of resources can exceed what would be a maximizing (only error-correcting) reallocation, but with none of the individual entrepreneurs responsible for causing the error.

The resource can also be allocated to one or many other production processes, which affects their value output and thus the value contributions of those resources. In other words, it can be the case that many entrepreneurs consider a resource to be overallocated to some production process A and act to reallocate that resource from A to many different production processes. Or vice versa, that they reallocate a resource from many different production processes to a single one that they consider to be underutilized.

In other words, albeit entrepreneurs aim to benefit from correcting existent "errors" (misallocations) in the economy (cf. Kirzner 1978), their actions may not in effect have an equilibrating outcome – individually or collectively – but can generate new errors (misallocations that cause discrepancies in returns).

Fourth, we cannot expect entrepreneurs to only respond to already existent and uncovered misallocations. Instead, we should expect entrepreneurs to act on their expectations. There are two reasons for this. First, whoever predicts and acts on a misallocation before it is revealed in market prices will be able to beat other entrepreneurs, who fail to make the prediction, to the punch. As a result, stepping ahead of the available information through, for example, price discrepancies can provide the entrepreneur with greater returns. Second, as the third point above suggests, as several entrepreneurs can (and probably will) respond to an uncovered opportunity for gains, they may in turn cause new misallocations. When this is so, an entrepreneur can increase their gains by counter-allocating the resource. The sooner this opportunity is discovered – or, better yet, predicted – the greater the potential gain.

Misallocations may therefore be corrected, at least to some extent, before they are discoverable. In other words, entrepreneurs have little to gain from passively waiting and then responding to return discrepancies that have already been realized. Such opportunities, to the extent that they arise and are not already in the process of being corrected, are short-lived at best. Any one entrepreneur is more likely to gain (and earn greater and more lasting returns) if they can correctly second-guess where returns will be higher and allocate the resource to take advantage of the gains before others discover the opportunity.

Fifth, as the previous points indicate, this process of error correction is not a unidirectional flow: entrepreneurs gain from reallocating productive resources from overallocated to underallocated uses but mistakes, made individually or collectively, can cause new misallocations. But is there an overall tendency in this process? Yes, because there are gains from correctly anticipating and acting on misallocations of a resource, we should expect each resource to over time find its way not only to better uses but also into the more capable hands. Those entrepreneurs who suffer losses must cover those by selling resources to those who earn positive returns. In other words, this market is equilibrating in its overall tendency even though it may not be in each reallocation.

As a result, the economy gets ever closer to general equilibrium, which is here defined as *allocative efficiency* – all resources are used where their value output is maximized. Will the economy reach this point? Yes, because there are no changing circumstances.[4] Consequently, there is no moving target and every improvement in the resource allocation is a permanent gain.

Note, however, that this process is not necessarily Pareto optimal as it is guided by total value output but does not imply that every entrepreneurial reallocation leaves each entrepreneur better off. In other words, some entrepreneurs will gain, while others may suffer losses. But the long-term trend of the market is to create more value for consumers.

2.2 Model 2: Exogenous Change

Model 2 takes what we learned from Model 1 and adds the possibility of exogenous change. Whereas entrepreneurs are still, as in Model 1, in the business of effecting new resource allocations between existing production processes, value production may be affected by changes that are outside the control of entrepreneurs' allocative efforts. These changes involve the available supply of resources, from discovery of new sources to the destruction wrought by natural disasters, and, importantly, consumer preferences (their rankings of consumer goods offered for sale).

Note that we do not yet include changes of endogenous origin, that is, changes to production caused by entrepreneurs themselves other than their efforts to (re)allocate resources between production processes. We will add endogenous change in Model 3. We here focus on the implications of allowing changes of exogenous origin.

Entrepreneurs in Model 2 allocate resources in a market environment in which the structure of value outcomes changes over time (in other words, supply and consumers' value rankings change). For the individual entrepreneur, this means gains from resource reallocations in the present are not and cannot be expected to be permanent. As a result, entrepreneurs must constantly reassess their allocations in pursuit of profits (and to avoid losses). Market efficiency (general equilibrium) is a moving target (cf. Kirzner 1973).

Thus, in addition to Model 1's problem of entrepreneurs exhausting an opportunity for gain by (over-)allocating resources to a particular production

---

[4] For simplicity, we here do not consider the impact of transaction costs, which could, in the Coasean (1937, 1960) interpretation, keep the economy from reaching its perfect maximum. (See, however, Demsetz (2011) on how the Coasean model may be mistaken and Bylund (2021) for an elaboration.)

process, the value potential of that process may unexpectedly change. This nonpermanence of gains increases the urgency with which entrepreneurs must effect resource reallocations to earn profits. This means that the advantage of acting on expectations instead of responding to already revealed opportunities increases. An entrepreneur who manages to allocate resources to where gains *will* arise, such as adding productive capacity to a production process that consumers will prefer, has a leg up on competitors and can thus capture much of the gains.

The truth of this becomes obvious when we recognize that resource allocation is not a mere mathematical exercise – it is not instantaneous – but an action that takes place in real time. As it takes time (and effort) to move a resource from one use to the next, which was also the case in Model 1, the circumstances can change before the resource is put to its new use. This is true also, albeit to a lesser extent, for unspecific, for example, highly standardized, resources (if any). In order to realize gains, therefore, which necessitates allocating resources in better ways (or earlier) than competitors, an entrepreneur has no choice but to make allocative decisions based on expectations and foresight. Entrepreneurship cannot here be merely responsive to opportunities that emerge in the market data.

Note that the opportunities for reallocating resources, as is the case also in Model 1, are limited to existing production processes. Entrepreneurs in Model 2 deal with a closed set of possibilities. While circumstances for production may change, the processes that make up the economic production structure will not – only their utilization and value output will. Entrepreneurs are thus still in the business of allocating resources from one line of production to the other.[5] This model thus largely complies with what has previously been called "dynamic efficiency" (e.g., Huerta De Soto 2008).[6] Kirzner explains this process in terms of the alertness of entrepreneurs:

> What is important is that, in operating along this dimension, entrepreneurial alertness is not only pushing prices towards relevant "equality", it is also *moving resources from one line of production to another*. The tendency, in a market economy, for resources to become reallocated from less productive uses (as judged by consumers) towards more productive uses, operates through the same entrepreneurial discovery procedure which creates a tendency for the prices of a given commodity to move towards equality. (Kirzner 1997, 42; emphasis in original)

---

[5] For simplicity, we assume in Model 2 that all existing production processes will always remain economically viable (retain sufficient demand to continue production). Were this not the case, the number of production processes, and with them the variety of consumer goods, would decrease over time (see Bylund 2018).

[6] For a recent critical assessment of dynamic efficiency, see Bylund (2024).

Kirzner elaborates on the economic implications and what they mean:

> The social advantages thus achieved do not constitute "social optimality" as defined from the perspective of imagined omniscience. They constitute instead a co-ordinative process during which market participants become aware of mutually beneficial opportunities for trade and, in grasping these opportunities, move to correct the earlier errors. (Kirzner 1997, 67)

To summarize our findings thus far, Model 2 differs from Model 1 only in that it, by assumption, allows for exogenous changes to the circumstances for production. As potential gains from resource reallocation are not permanent but may expire with changing supply of inputs or consumer preferences, we expect entrepreneurs to shift their decision-making from responsive to expectational. The greater urgency to exploit the potentially short-lived opportunities for gain suggests all entrepreneurs rely primarily on their expectations.

The reason for this conclusion becomes clear if we elaborate on the decision calculus for entrepreneurs in the respective models. In Model 1, each gain exists for as long as it remains underexploited. It will not be exhausted other than through other entrepreneurs' reallocative actions. In other words, any entrepreneur can capture part of the gains by acting on a revealed opportunity if they believe that they can reallocate their resources swiftly enough (faster than other entrepreneurs). There is no uncertainty as to the gain itself – the opportunity exists and is readily discoverable.

Consequently, the cost of acting not on a discovered opportunity but on expectations that an inefficient allocation of resources will be (but is not yet) revealed, and presuming that one can proactively reallocate resources to exploit that opportunity, is comparatively high in Model 1. It in effect constitutes shifting one's actions from risk to uncertainty (Knight 1921; Packard, Clark, and Klein 2017): the probability of being slower than necessary to exploit an existing opportunity versus the uncertainty of when and where there will be opportunities for gain that can be proactively exploited.

In Model 2, an opportunity for gain is still objectively existing, but it is not limited only by the degree it has been fully exploited. Here, the opportunity does not last until exhausted and it does not arise due only to previous entrepreneurial "errors." Revealed opportunities for gains may occur and expire before any resources have been (re)allocated to it. In other words, the time it takes one entrepreneur to reallocate their resources from other production processes, relative to the time it takes other entrepreneurs to do the same, is only one of the limitations. The nature, magnitude, and existence of the potential gain may change due to exogenous factors.

To reiterate, in Model 2 it is not enough to beat other entrepreneurs to a discovered opportunity because this may still not earn a gain if circumstances change. Similarly, (mis)allocating resources to a production process where there is no present (and thus no yet discoverable) opportunity for gain can still create gains for the entrepreneur – if, for example, exogenous changes shift demand to this process, thereby making the current allocation of resources into a relative underallocation (and thus there are gains from shifting resources to it). In other words, the future state and value of Model 2 market production is uncertain, not merely risky.

This changes the decision calculus for entrepreneurs by significantly increasing the cost of the lower-cost strategy in Model 1 (responding to discovered opportunities). It is no longer merely risky but requires uncertainty-bearing and thus the potential for error. Gains are not permanent and may expire even if they are not fully exhausted, and competing entrepreneurs should, on the margin, to a greater extent base their resource allocations on expectations, both of which increase the chances that responsive entrepreneurs are too late to capture gains.

In other words, in Model 2 much more than in Model 1, entrepreneurs should for their resource allocations be expected to rely on judgment (e.g., Knight 1921; McMullen 2015; Packard and Bylund forthcoming), imagination (e.g., Shackle 1979; Gartner 2007), and other means for forming expectations about the future (e.g., Lachmann 1943, 1945, 1982).

2.3 Model 3: Endogenous Change

Model 3 removes the final category of simplifying assumptions: endogenously generated change. Whereas Models 1 and 2 focused on allocating productive resources between already existing production processes, thus affecting their respective output quantities, Model 3 allows entrepreneurs to create *new* value by establishing novel production processes and producing new consumer goods.

In Model 3, entrepreneurs can and do still allocate resources to (and from) production processes already in existence. However, they may also creatively bring about "new combinations" of resources, to again use Schumpeter's (1934) preferred term, to replace or increase the output quantity of a production process or produce a new consumer good.[7] (We will return to and discuss Schumpeter's combinations in greater detail in Section 3.3.)

---

[7] This innovative, new-value creative entrepreneur is responsible for the "creative destruction" of market production (Schumpeter 1947) and is known in the literature under many names, for example, entrepreneur-promoter (Mises 1998), capitalist-entrepreneur (Böhm-Bawerk 1959; Rothbard 2004), and integral entrepreneur (Salerno 2008).

The possibility of entrepreneur-caused new value creation (endogenous change) changes the nature of the economy's dynamics, and therefore also the situation for entrepreneurs (Bylund 2022a). As Bylund (2024) argues, the market process subject to entrepreneurially caused endogenous change – entrepreneurial innovation in pursuit of new value creation – goes well beyond dynamic efficiency (Huerta De Soto 2008). The market process is not obviously or consistently equilibrating as new value is pursued and created under uncertainty but is nevertheless consistently *progressing* in value terms.

Let us briefly look at the implications of endogenous change for errors, value production, uncertainty, and entrepreneurial strategies.

Errors. The nature of "error" in the economy has changed as we have relaxed our initially strong assumptions. In Model 1, error was the inefficient use of a productive resource from the perspective of (reachable) general equilibrium. This meant that any error correction is a permanent gain as it produces a lasting improvement in the economy's overall value outcome. (This does not imply that entrepreneurial profits are permanent, however, since entrepreneurial reallocations exhaust a correction's gains.)

Model 2 introduced the possibility of changing circumstances such that exogenous changes shift production maximum. As a result, previous productions and improvements made to the resource allocation may become misaligned with the new, post-shift market equilibrium. Thus, errors are as objective as in Model 1, but are temporary as they last only until circumstances change and new errors (misallocations) therefore arise.

In Model 3, entrepreneurs can introduce new errors to the overall production structure by speculatively establishing new production processes that they expect to create greater value outcome. In other words, these entrepreneurs discover[8] a new and previously unknown value potential of existing resources (in new combinations) that, as a result, make other entrepreneurs' productions misaligned and inefficient. The difference to Model 2 is that one entrepreneur can here, by successfully innovating, impose errors onto other entrepreneurs, whereas in Model 2 all entrepreneurs were subject to, and "recipients" of, errors imposed by changing circumstances.

Value production. Our analysis of value output in the different models follows from the nature of their respective types of errors. Model 1 over time

---

[8] The word "discover," as commonly used to describe entrepreneurial speculation, suggests that what is discovered already exist, but this is not here the case: The potential for new value is entirely subjective and imagined by the entrepreneur. With the power of hindsight, we might say that entrepreneurs discovered new ways of creating value, but when investment and production decisions are made, there is, as we argued in previous sections, no information or knowledge available about the actual value potential of an action. See the discussion in Section 3.

increases its value production as entrepreneurs correct errors but no new errors are introduced. Economic progress here entails a consistent and incremental process that eventually will reach a state of general equilibrium. In Model 2 the improvements are discontinuous and value output can temporarily fall as changing circumstances shift productive maximum. This means there should be more opportunities for profit for entrepreneurs, but also that its total value production, assuming there is a value metric, lags that of Model 1. Model 2 is constantly "disequilibrated" (the "distance" to equilibrium increases) as circumstances change and previously accurately allocations of resources may become misallocated.

For Model 3, the set of possibilities for new value creation that entrepreneurs may attempt is limited to their creativity and imagination although the theoretical absolute limit for value creation is (remains) the full contentment of consumers. Successful innovations generate profits to the entrepreneurs to the degree the innovation facilitates new value that, at least to some extent, can be captured. In practical terms, therefore, there are little or no limits to value production.

Uncertainty. Model 1 includes little uncertainty about opportunities because they are objective and observable as price discrepancies. However, for each individual entrepreneur, there is uncertainty regarding the degree to which they will be able to exploit an opportunity. This, in turn, is determined by the extent of resource reallocations by other entrepreneurs. In Model 2, there is also uncertainty regarding exogenous changes and the effect they might have on the focal entrepreneur's resource allocation. The reallocations by other entrepreneurs, which we expect to be anticipatory of rather than responsive to opportunities, add further uncertainty about the potential value of any individual entrepreneur's resource allocation. Yet the opportunity is objective for the limited time that it exists.

In Model 3, the uncertainty borne by an entrepreneur is primarily resultant from the *actions of other entrepreneurs*. It emanates from the possibility that another entrepreneur may attempt and succeed in innovating new value creation that affects (undermines), directly or indirectly, the profitability of existing resource allocations. In other words, uncertainty about the ability to exploit an existing opportunity, observable in the market data in the present, is in Model 3 vastly overshadowed by the uncertainty wrought by other entrepreneurs. What was exploitable errors and thus opportunities for profit in Models 1 and 2 may not be so in Model 3 as there may already be new value creation projects underway that will undermine or make irrelevant those errors – and therefore the potential profit earned from correcting them.

This uncertainty of the future conditions of the market, augmented by entrepreneurial speculations on new value creation, has substantial implications for what are appropriate entrepreneurial strategies.

Entrepreneurial strategies. In Model 1, in which opportunities are objective and observable, the appropriate strategy is to stay alert and act swiftly as an opportunity arises. The more responsive the entrepreneur, the quicker off their feet, the greater the chance for profit. We noted above that entrepreneurs may attempt to second-guess where and when the next price discrepancy will arise but found that the costs of doing so are very high – the chances and cost of getting it wrong would typically outweigh the chances for greater profits. This changes in Model 2, where opportunities are objective but subject to (mostly) unforeseeable exogenous changes and, therefore, the relative cost of responding to (rather than attempting to anticipate) opportunities increases. As a result, the appropriate strategy may be to attempt to predict where opportunities (under- or misallocations) may arise.

In Model 3, the introduction of endogenous change – disruption wrought by innovative, new-value creative entrepreneurship – suggests that treating opportunities as exogenous poses a significant cost on the entrepreneur. To relate this shift to the discourse in academic entrepreneurship journals, we have moved from Model 1 and 2's "discovery opportunities" (Venkataraman 1997; Shane 2003), which exist or can be perceived in the market data (cf. Kirzner 1973), to a conception more akin to "creation opportunities" that are enacted by the entrepreneur (Alvarez and Barney 2007).[9] The appropriate strategies in Model 1 and 2, in which the entrepreneur either chooses to respond to opportunities as they arise or attempts to second-guess where and when they do so, no longer apply. The reason for this is that Model 3 does not present a resource allocation that can be improved by simple reallocation between processes.

To see this, we need only consider the situation of a maximized resource allocation in which each resource is used where it produces the most value output. Even if we for a moment disregard the exogenous changes introduced in Model 2, which would necessitate reshuffling of resources to maintain production maximum, the maximizing allocation can at any time be disrupted by an entrepreneur innovating to create new value for consumers (Christensen, Raynor, and McDonald 2015). Consequently, even allocation of one's resources in the direction of what is value output maximum in current production

---

[9] It should be stressed that while our conception of opportunities for profit in Models 1 and 2 in many ways bears resemblance with discovery opportunities, our conception of Model 3 entrepreneurship deviates from and goes beyond creation opportunities. This will become obvious as we elaborate on this model in Section 3.

processes may still not generate profits in the face of the uncertainty caused by potential new value creation.

This suggests that any entrepreneur must choose one of two options, both of which require uncertainty-bearing beyond what was possible in Model 1 and 2. One option is to attempt to disrupt through innovating, which is a highly uncertain undertaking and may not create new value or generate profits. After all, most entrepreneurs fail most of the time.[10] On the other hand, if the innovation is successful, the innovative entrepreneur can reasonably expect to capture significant profits as part of their new value creation.

The other option is to act under the assumption (or hope) that an existent opportunity will not soon be disrupted so that profits can be captured. This strategy is perhaps less demanding of the individual entrepreneur, who will not need to speculate on how to create new value. But the ability to earn profits here depends entirely on the competition (how many other entrepreneurs act to exploit the same opportunity) and the opportunity is limited to whether and when it will be undermined by innovations. In other words, this seemingly "safer" option, which does not aim to create new value for future consumers, does not avoid the uncertainty of disruption but must bear it without effecting it. Change can be expected, both in what productions are undertaken and which ones create sufficient value to be viable. The entrepreneur must either actively meet the future (create new value) or passively endure it.

These strategies largely capture the difference between what Koellinger (2008) calls innovative and imitative entrepreneurship and that Sautet (2013) refers to as systemic and local entrepreneurship, respectively.

In the next section, we will elaborate on the implications for entrepreneurship as well as the nature of the economy subject to entrepreneurial new value creation – the market process. As will become clear, the conception of entrepreneurship in Evolutionary Economics goes beyond Models 1 and 2 but does not fully recognize the implications of Model 3. Specifically, we will see that knowledge is not nearly as relevant as is commonly assumed.

3 The Entrepreneurial Market Process

The previous section introduced three models of market disequilibrium. We learned that because production is not perfectly aligned with satisfying consumer wants (disequilibrium), there are opportunities for economic gain from lessening such misalignment. To the degree that such improvements can be

---

[10] The Bureau of Labor Statistics keeps a table of private business survival rates in the United States at www.bls.gov/bdm/us_age_naics_00_table7.txt.

captured as profits, they motivate entrepreneurial action. For this reason, an economy in disequilibrium is best understood as a process.

We also saw that entrepreneurship as simple arbitrage, or the correction of misalignments by reallocating productive resources between production processes, suggests a consistent equilibrating tendency. In Model 1, entrepreneurial actions exploit such opportunities for profit and produce a market process that is continuously equilibrating and will eventually establish equilibrium.

In Model 2, which introduced changing circumstances, equilibrium is no longer a fixed point but a moving target. Production processes that are aligned with the prevailing conditions can become misaligned as conditions change and thus present new opportunities for corrections. Entrepreneurial action remains equilibrating as it profits from correcting misalignments – whether acting in response to existing opportunities or anticipating new ones – but the changing circumstances suggest that the market process overall is not continuously and consistently closing in on equilibrium. The equilibration of the market process becomes a cat-and-mouse game.

The nature of the market process changes when we allow entrepreneurs to not only respond to circumstances, existing or expected, but creatively pursue new value creation. This is what we did in Model 3 and we will now elaborate on the implications for the market process.

3.1 Equilibrium versus Knowledge Problem

The market process implied by Model 3, in which we allow entrepreneurs to pursue new value creation, is different from those implied by Model 1 and 2 (Bylund 2022a, 2024). It goes beyond the corrections of misalignments in existing production processes. Whereas entrepreneurs still allocate productive resources, profit opportunities are no longer limited to effecting improvements to the alignment of existing production processes. Instead, imaginative entrepreneurs may anticipate that there are greater profit opportunities in creating new goods and services that, they expect, will better serve consumers.

Allowing for entrepreneurial creation of new value, which causes changes to the production structure endogenously, shifts the meaning of equilibrium and ultimately reverses the direction of causality generating the market process.

Let us first consider equilibrium. In Model 1, equilibrium constitutes maximum value production through the full utilization of existing resources: allocative efficiency. This is accomplished by aligning resource use in existing production processes with consumer wants. Equilibrium is full alignment. In Model 2, equilibrium can be similarly defined but is here a moving target as circumstances (both supply of resources and consumer wants) change. Unless exogenous changes cease, allocative efficiency cannot be reached. But the process of constant entrepreneurial reallocation of resources suggests entrepreneurs typically cause Pareto improvements and that the process engendered is constituted by dynamic efficiency (Huerta De Soto 2008; cf. Bylund 2024).

In both models, there is no difference at any point in time between the maximum value output of the existing production structure and the potential maximum value output of the economy's production. Both are equal to allocative efficiency, although in Model 2, it is not a fixed point but a moving target.

In Model 3, what constitutes maximum value production in existing production processes is *not* the potential maximum value output. Full production implies the full utilization of existing resources in existing production processes. But as entrepreneurs can imagine new ways of creating (more) value for consumers, it is possible to create greater value than the goods produced under maximum resource utilization in existing production processes – the productions possibilities frontier can be shifted out through endogenous (entrepreneurial) novel production undertakings.

Thus, as Schumpeter recognizes, entrepreneurship "incessantly revolutionizes the economic structure *from within*, incessantly destroying the old one, incessantly creating a new one" (Schumpeter 1947, 83, emphasis in original).

What is of interest here (we will return to the details of endogenous changes to production below) is that entrepreneurial new value creation separates the present production maximum from the potential value maximum. The former is a matter of efficiency in resource allocation (allocative efficiency or Pareto optimality), which depends on the degree to which actors in the economy have knowledge of what value can be created using existing resources. Indeed, disequilibrium as it is defined in Model 1 and 2 is fundamentally a knowledge problem: efficiency (equilibrium) would be attainable with knowledge of what resource allocation would maximize value output.[11]

To use Model 1 as illustration, if entrepreneurs had knowledge of their respective resources' maximizing use(s), they would allocate them accordingly and as a result bring about equilibrium. Equilibration would then be a very swift process and would neither require a stepwise process of error correction nor include potential errors such as over-allocation of a resource to a specific use. Similarly in Model 2, equilibrium would, at least in theory, be quickly established after each exogenous change if entrepreneurs have knowledge of each resource's new maximizing use. There is no reason to expect entrepreneurs to make errors or fail to correct previously existing errors, if any, completely.

---

[11] Although simple models in economics exclude entrepreneurship, they are often compatible with entrepreneurship as opportunity discovery (e.g., Kirzner 1973).

Note that this knowledge problem is not a matter of technology but of resource allocation, which entrepreneurs bring about in their aim to earn profits. As Mises (1998, 300) puts it, "the problem we have in mind differs from the technological tasks of the technicians" because entrepreneurial "decisions must be effected in such a way as to prefer that solution of the problem which ... is the most economical one." In other words, entrepreneurs determine and are rewarded for effecting the *economizing* use of resources in production. Technology (and technological knowledge) is a constraint, but technological efficiency does not determine economic efficiency.

Model 3 shifts the upper limit beyond allocative efficiency in resource use to imagined but uncertain new value creation. The former, which constituted maximum in Model 1 and 2, offers a limited (constrained) set of possibilities, whereas the latter for all practical purposes is an open set. The former is consequently primarily a world of risk while the latter is one of "Knightian" uncertainty (Knight 1921).

3.2 New Value Creation

The potential value maximum in Model 3 is not limited by allocation of resources toward their efficient use in existing production processes. As the production structure can be reimagined and new types of goods and production processes attempted by entrepreneurs, neither allocative efficiency nor dynamic efficiency poses upper bounds for the value output (Bylund 2024). Instead, the economy's value-productive capability is limited by the creativity and imagination of entrepreneurs seeking to profit from finding new ways to serve consumers.[12]

The important implication here is the uncertainty that follows from the fact that production takes time. As we noted in Section 2.3, value is created only ex post by and for consumers and therefore new production commenced in the present must be of unknown value.[13] Consequently, when the value of a produced good is realized, through consumers buying and using the good, it is too late to adjust production to this fact. Production precedes consumption.

It may also be too late for others to mimic or emulate the production process that turned out to be successful (profitable) because when their products become available to consumers, it is quite possible that innovative entrepreneurs have already found ways to create new value. In other words, the opportunity that

---

[12] In theory, the absolute limit is the full contentment of consumers, but this is impossible because it implies a world without scarcity. (Scarcity is here understood in the economic sense of having less of something than there are valuable uses for that something.)

[13] This uncertainty does not apply in Model 1 as consumer valuations do not change. Whereas it applies in Model 2, it does so only to a very limited extent as only consumers' preference rankings of existent goods change.

was observable *because it was created by previous innovations* may already have been undermined and supplanted. This is why imitative entrepreneurship, as we noted in the previous section, is not in Model 3 a safe strategy: the potential for profit from responding to already realized profit opportunities can be undermined by entrepreneurs aiming for new value creation. Entrepreneurs who already have the resources on hand (or can acquire them) and imitate the profitable production process quickly may be able to capture some of the profits, but they cannot count on the opportunity being permanent and may have to share profits with other imitators.

Whereas entrepreneurship, especially innovative such, is sometimes made out to be about throwing things at the wall to "see what sticks," it is not random and therefore not purely about luck (cf. Demsetz 1983). New value creation is cumulative and intentional, but not only in terms of technology – knowledge of possibilities can and do inspire and motivate new innovations that further change market conditions. This is easy to see if we recognize that the uncertainty-bearing of entrepreneurs is fundamentally about the ability to imagine the future state of the market – and how best to exploit it. As in any state of the market, the prospect of selling one's good at a price in excess of cost depends on the supply of substitutes and other valuable goods made available to consumers and market demand for this type of goods. In other words, it is a matter of offering as much value as possible compared to what other entrepreneurs will offer (Bylund 2019).

As value is subjective, new value creation is facilitated by empathizing with the intended consumer – to attempt to accurately place oneself in their shoes and anticipate how they can best be served (McMullen 2015). As production possibilities are limited by technology, it also comes down to being able to accurately predict and assess different adjacent possibles (Koppl et al. 2023). However, whereas technological possibilities limit what can be done and how, technological savvy provides no insight into the economic (value-based) ranking of those possibilities.

Indeed, Schumpeter (1947, 132) wrote that "the function of entrepreneurs is to reform or revolutionize the pattern of production by exploiting an invention or, more generally, an untried technological possibility for producing a new commodity or producing an old one in a new way." But this comes close to confusing two distinct phenomena, which Schumpeter himself recognized: one that refers to technology and one that is economic. The invention is the novel technology, whereas the entrepreneur *innovates* – brings new ideas to market and makes them valuable. An innovation can be based on and leverage an invention, but this is not necessarily the case. Mises stressed this difference between technology and economy:

> Technology tells how a given end could be attained by the employment of various means which can be used together in various combinations, or how

various available means could be employed for certain purposes. But it is at a loss to tell man which procedures he should choose out of the infinite variety of imaginable and possible modes of production. What acting man wants to know is how he must employ the available means for the best possible – the most economic – removal of felt uneasiness. (Mises 1998, 208)

What "most economic" means is "most value-creative," and we thus find that future market conditions, in both supply and demand, ultimately consist of people, their valuations and actions: consumers to serve and other entrepreneurs whose competing value offerings must be outdone.

In other words, the future is not random but is intentional and human. As Ludwig M. Lachmann puts it,

> The future is unknowable, though not unimaginable. Future knowledge cannot be had now, but it can cast its shadow ahead. In each mind, however, the shadow assumes a different shape, hence the divergence of expectations. The formation of expectations is an act of our mind by means of which we try to catch a glimpse of the unknown. Each one of us catches a different glimpse. (Lachmann 1976, 59)

Entrepreneurs aiming to facilitate as much value as possible for consumers are not limited to what production processes are already in place, other than indirectly through their production of necessary inputs. They are also not limited to what goods and services, real or imagined, consumers say that they want. The apocryphal statement by Henry Ford that "had I asked my customers what they wanted, they would have said faster horses" elegantly illustrates this. Very often consumers do not know what they want until they are shown the finished good. As a result, entrepreneurs must attempt to place themselves in the consumer's shoes and imagine what they might value. We will return to the greater implications of value-orientedness in Section 3.5 below, but it is sufficient here to recognize that it means entrepreneurs in the present compete with each other based on *the value they expect to offer consumers in the future.*

This means the already established production processes – the production structure currently serving consumers – is the result of what entrepreneurs previously guessed would be of greatest value for consumers, which in turn may be unrelated to what entrepreneurs in the present imagine will be most valuable. Indeed, "all production processes are invariably prospective" (Huerta De Soto 2009, 298).

The efficiency of an existing production structure, by which we mean how close it is to the full utilization of resources in production given the present state of knowledge – allocative efficiency – does *not* direct production. It is *entrepreneurial imagination* that directs production and the aim and intended outcome is to create new value for future consumers. The imaginative entrepreneur acting to earn profits from new value creation is the driving force of the market process (Bylund 2020).

3.3 The Meaning of Disruption

Schumpeter, the "prophet of innovation" (McCraw 2007), explains that economic development is brought about by "the carrying out of new combinations" by entrepreneurs (Schumpeter 1934, 66). He contrasts this with regular or continued production, which "combine[s] materials and forces within our reach" (Schumpeter 1934, 65), thereby stressing that development – the higher standard of living brought about by increased production – is about *new* combinations. He identifies five ways (he calls them "cases") in which value output can be increased and thus contribute to raising the standard of living:

(1) The introduction of a new good ... or of a new quality of a good
(2) The introduction of a new method of production
(3) The opening of a new market
(4) The conquest of a new source of supply of raw materials or half-manufactured goods
(5) The carrying out of the new organisation of any industry (Schumpeter 1934, 66)

Whereas all of these "cases" increase the market's total value output, and therefore contribute to economic development, we are here interested in only the first two. The reason is that the other cases address increased production quantity without changing the production processes – much like we discussed in Models 1 and 2 above.

Our interest here, in line with Model 3, is in the endogenous change to the production structure, which facilitates new value creation. Cases 1 and 2 largely represent new value creation by creating and implementing a new technology (broadly understood) or by applying already existing technologies in new ways. Both amount to innovation or making new ideas (inventions) valuable through, as Schumpeter puts it, creating a new good or using new production methods.

However, it should be noted that case 1 is new-value creative only to the extent it implies structural novelty in production. New goods that can be produced by a simple rearrangement of existing resources contribute little novelty as they are previously unused combinations of standard components, like LEGO pieces put together in a different order. Whereas this formally is a new combination of components, it entails mere reallocation rather than endogenous change and can be very easily mimicked or emulated.

Schumpeter appears to agree with this limitation when referring to regular production (as opposed to new combinations) as "combin[ing] materials and forces within our reach" (Schumpeter 1934, 65). New combinations in the sense of new value creation would require more than this. We should nevertheless not make too much of this theoretical possibility as it is mostly an issue of conceptual demarcation. In reality, very few new goods of value to consumers can be produced without also requiring a case-2 change. Case 1 therefore, from our new-value creative perspective, all but collapses into and can be treated as case 2.

In contrast, cases 3–5 are *not* about creating new value. Case 3 is a matter of extending the reach of already existing production, for example, by introducing an existing product in a new country or to a new demographic. Simply put, it is about meeting existing but previously unexploited or underserved demand and is therefore largely compatible with our Models 1 and 2.

Case 4 is a matter of exogenous change on the supply side, which we covered in Model 2. Increased supply of inputs certainly facilitates increased production quantities, but this implies only greater throughput in existing production processes using existing technological knowledge. It may, in turn, require reallocation of resources between processes, but it does not entail "new combinations."

Similarly with case 5, which suggests increased total production quantity through a different organization of production units. This case is about the administration and direction of production facilities in an industry (i.e., market structure), not about changing production processes.[14] As Schumpeter puts it, "the creation of a monopoly position (for example through trustification) or the breaking up of a monopoly position" (1934, 66). This is a change as to how present production processes are organized but does not imply "new combinations" in production.

The implications of Schumpeter's cases 1 and 2 require further elaboration. As we noted in our discussion in Section 3.2, new value creation goes beyond reallocation of resources and, consequently, the correcting of discovered errors or adjusting production quantities to known or anticipated changes in circumstances. Our conception of endogenous change – entrepreneurial new value creation – entails an entrepreneurially driven change to the economy's

---

[14] The impact of novel organizing of production, as opposed to the structure of organizations administrating production facilities and processes, should not be underestimated. But this is covered by Schumpeter's case 2.

production structure (and, as a result, its value output). It is therefore instructive to look at its "disruptive" implications.[15]

It should be stressed again that in new value creation it is not the novelty that makes the value: it is the value, imagined or anticipated, that justifies the novelty. Indeed, it is the entrepreneur's belief that they can create new value, and that this offers them an opportunity for profit, that motivates them to attempt something new (a new good or production method – or both).

Although the individual entrepreneur may be aiming merely at the potential for earning profits in excess of what is possible in existing production processes, the systemic effects are of fundamental importance. Successful entrepreneurial new value creation breaks new ground in terms of productive capabilities *of existing resources* and, as a consequence, shifts the boundary of value production (Bylund 2015a; 2022a). This is not a matter of invention (new technology and/or knowledge) but innovation. In other words, the innovative entrepreneur, by disrupting the existing production structure, pushes the point of allocative efficiency in value terms outward, much like Schumpeter (1934, 1947) theorized.

The meaning of endogenous change therefore becomes clear. It differs from mere allocation of resources between existing production processes, whether or not made in response to (or anticipation of) changing circumstances, because it increases the value productive capability of existing resources by introducing, as in Schumpeter's cases 1 and 2, new types of goods or new ways of producing them. In both cases, the restructuring of production releases previously unknown and unanticipated – and for the entrepreneur unknowable but imaginable – productive capability.

As this takes place within an economy that already has an established production structure, perhaps as a type of "circular flow" of production (Schumpeter 1934), new value creation entails an attempt to replace (outcompete) some existing production process. To Evolutionary Economics, and specifically the neo-Schumpeterian theory of the firm, this is about technology: "[t]he entrepreneur is the leader who leads the firm to new techniques" (Winter 2006, 136). But from a value-creative perspective, which Model 3 necessitates, this is not a matter of learning new techniques or adopting new technology, but

---

[15] Disruption, or the introduction of disruptive innovation, is formally defined as "a process whereby a smaller company with fewer resources is able to successfully challenge established incumbent businesses" (Christensen, Raynor, and McDonald 2015) by making a breakthrough with technologies that "look financially unattractive to established companies" (Bower and Christensen 1995) yet that changes an industry's competitive patterns. We will here use it in the colloquial (broader) sense of market-changing, new-value creative innovation.

to speculate on new types of production that are of unknown value. In other words, it is *entrepreneurship*.

Bylund (2016) analyzes in detail how entrepreneurs in specialized economies can create new value. Their novel production process(es) in pursuit of new value creation establish "islands of specialization" that utilize and benefit from new (more intensive) divisions of labor. This does not require firms or necessarily take place in firms but *constitutes* the firm. The entrepreneur's novel production is, economically speaking, naturally integrated as the structure is internally interdependent and its division of labor largely independent of the external market.

Rarely do entrepreneurs create new value by establishing an entire supply chain from original factors to consumer goods. Instead, especially in advanced and highly specialized economies, they rely on markets for intermediate goods (inputs and/or outputs) and so must in their innovations (1) remain compatible with the existing production structure while (2) challenging existing production processes by doing things differently (Bylund 2020). This suggests that the entrepreneurial firm, which consists in the implementation of the entrepreneur's innovative production, either succeeds or fails as a whole – it is the firm, not its constitutive parts, that earns a profit or suffers a loss. The entrepreneur must thus bear the uncertainty of the venture until (and if) it generates revenue.

Within the entrepreneurial firm, knowledge of what technology works (and how well it works) will be generated through engaging in trial and error and with experience. However, this knowledge refers to the effectiveness of the production process only – it is technological knowledge – and not to the value of what is produced. After the fact, when the entrepreneur has earned a profit or suffered a loss, knowledge of what was the right productive investment (the innovation) is generated – but it refers only to the specific past in which it was made. Whether the same reasoning will apply also to the production of the same goods to be offered for sale *in the future* is again speculation. The *value* of production, which will always be realized only after the fact, is always uncertain and therefore entrepreneurial.

From our perspective, then, it is difficult to agree with Schumpeter:

> What has been done already has the sharp-edged reality of all the things which we have seen and experienced; the new is only the figment of our imagination. Carrying out a new plan and acting according to a customary one are things as different as making a road and walking along it. (Schumpeter 1934, 85)

However, Schumpeter's words ring true if we look to the effectiveness of the production process rather than the efficiency (value) of it. It is certainly the case that the "carrying out of a plan," in the sense of managing the production process to maximize quantity produced, is a matter of technology, and therefore of knowledge. The specifics and effectiveness of new production processes are (much) less known than processes that already exist. But the value of the output is not a function of the effectiveness of the production process; it remains unknown because the actual demand for the good depends on those specific future market conditions. Thus, the entrepreneur must continuously bear the uncertainty of production (we will discuss uncertainty in the next section). The decisions to commence, continue, and cease production are entrepreneurial.

On the system level, the success of a single attempted disruption – a new, more productive organizing of production as an "island of specialization" (Bylund 2016) or Schumpeterian new production method (Schumpeter 1934) – changes the value basis for allocative entrepreneurship. The problems solved by dynamic efficiency (see Model 2 above and Bylund (2024)), in which entrepreneurs seek to improve resource allocations between existing production processes under the uncertainty of changing circumstances (supply and demand for existing production processes), are themselves undermined by entrepreneurial revolutionizing of the production structure. In a sense, disruptive entrepreneurs can pull the rug from under the feet of those who are carrying out existing production processes and allocating resources between them. Bylund notes:

> it is the promoter's [innovative entrepreneur's] speculative undertaking of novel production processes and new ways of doing business that create the specific future market conditions under which all types of entrepreneurs can earn profits (or suffer losses). (Bylund 2020, 357)

3.4 Uncertainty

The intended result of new value creation for the entrepreneur is profit, that is, returns in excess of what can be anticipated through (re)allocating resources. However, the effect of introducing novelty into the market's production is systemic and affects other entrepreneurs as well. We noted in the previous section that it only takes one successful attempt at entrepreneurial new value creation to undermine the adjustment processes that make up Model 1 and 2: error correction toward allocative efficiency and dynamic efficiency, respectively.

However, future disruption cannot be predicted with precision because we cannot know consumers' responses to new goods (attempted new value creation) before the fact. This applies to *all* entrepreneurs. Even knowing what inventions are underway is insufficient to know the nature and impact (the value) of the innovations they might bring. Inventions, as already noted, are a matter of technology and thus primarily a knowledge problem, whereas innovations are a matter of bringing new ideas to the market and making them valuable. Innovations can, but need not, be based on invention, as shown by historic examples like Henry Ford's Model T – the affordable automobile that changed the world – and Gary Dahl's Pet Rock – the 1975 Christmas season fad of selling rocks as the "perfect" pet.

Just like the innovating entrepreneur cannot know but must imagine the value they bring to consumers, competing entrepreneurs also cannot know whether or to what extent their industry or niche may (or can) be disrupted. Competing entrepreneurs' strategy set is therefore limited to three main options. First, they can ignore the possibility and hope for the best. Whereas this implies little cost or preparatory action in the present, the extent of their profit-earning capability in face of disruption becomes a matter of luck (see e.g., Demsetz 1983; McCaffrey 2016).

Second, they can recognize the possibility of disruption and take preparatory action. Such preparations may involve information gathering such as scanning the market for inventions and potential innovations, keeping up to date with technological developments, monitoring the competition, and so on.[16] But it should also include investments to increase responsiveness such as measures to improve agility and thereby increase the chances of avoiding failure. The advantage compared to the previous strategy is that this should increase the likelihood of surviving disruption. The downside is the added cost of these measures, which reduces profitability, and that taking them still does not guarantee survival.

The third remaining strategy is to become an innovator and potential disruptor seeking to create sufficient new value to jump ahead of and disrupt the competition as well as other potential disruptors. The costs of this strategy are typically higher than for the other strategies (Schumpeter 1947), and there are no guarantees that attempted innovations are successful. However, the upside is also (much) greater.

Not only does disrupting production entail capturing *all* of the available profits but disruptions tend to be more than incremental, which could extend the life of the innovation's profitability. Bylund refers to the figurative distance between present production and disruptive innovation, in which novelty is easily realizable through market means, as an "infeasibility zone":

> all productive innovations that are impossible to realise through market means suffer from unknowability and that their internal strict interdependence suggests

---

[16] This is often taught in entrepreneurship courses as a technique for discovering opportunities for starting a new business (Barringer and Ireland 2019).

> incompleteness even from failure in one of their parts. Implementation of these innovations should therefore primarily take place for those that constitute radical rather than marginal change in the structure of production. (Bylund 2016, 100)

The third strategy may not be every entrepreneur's cup of tea; however, it is what defines the innovative entrepreneur: "his eagerness to make profits as large as possible" (Mises 1998, 256). The mere possibility of disruption implies that there is a chance that someone could; it is also an incentive to innovate and, therefore, increases the chance that others may find the third strategy most appropriate.

In any market that does not suffer complete control or stasis,[17] there is always a *chance* that production will be disrupted. We thus find that the mere *possibility* that someone may attempt innovations, and thus that it is possible to imagine potential gains from doing something novel, increases the chances that entrepreneurs will attempt to innovate. In other words, they may choose disruption as their strategy for survival: offense as the best defense, so to speak. Consequently, the market process cannot properly be characterized by continuous, incremental change. This appears to disqualify Models 1 and 2 as means for understanding real markets – they capture not the nature of the market but specific entrepreneurial strategies, which can be effective only under the presumption that no relevant innovation takes place.

As the value of undertaken production processes is determined after the fact – in the market conditions when and where the produced goods are sold – the very *possibility* of disruption and therefore unforeseen and unforeseeable circumstances makes every production undertaking uncertain. Importantly, it is not merely the fact that the future wants of consumers is unknown but also that their rankings of wants depends on the goods available to satisfy them: their presumed utility and efficacy in specific removal of felt uneasiness. In other words, whereas entrepreneurship constitutes uncertainty-bearing, the exercise of entrepreneurial production produces ("adds" to) the uncertainty that entrepreneurs must bear.

In conclusion, it is certainly the case that the market economy constantly evolves and unfolds, but we cannot assume that it does so evenly and incrementally. More likely, market progress happens spasmodically through attempts at entrepreneurial new value creation. It takes leaps forward with new ways to serve consumers, which are unknown and uncertain before they are approved by consumers choosing to buy the goods produced (Bylund 2011, 2016).

---

[17] "Complete control" here refers to a situation in which (1) no one has the means or capability to innovate, for example, if there is no private property, or (2) no one is allowed do so (assuming full compliance).

3.5 Economic Calculation

New value creation, despite being highly uncertain, is undertaken based on a simple calculus:

> value > price > cost

The entrepreneur imagines that the intended good – the innovation – will serve consumers more than alternative goods offered up for sale. In other words, it will be of high(er) value. This value determines the price the consumer is willing to pay. In order to buy the good, the consumer must consider the value received to be at least as high as the value they would expect from other uses of that amount of money (typically, another good in the present or the future).

For the consumer, therefore, the purchase decision is based on a value ranking of their different uses of an amount of money. The cost of buying one good is the value that could be attained from another good – the opportunity cost – which could also be bought using that amount of money. In other words, the consumer goes through with a purchase because it is where they expect the greatest gain in value terms.

For the entrepreneur (seller), the appropriate selling price must be low enough to provide the consumer with gain so that they will go through with the purchase. This limit, the upper bound of payable prices, is decided entirely by the consumer. The only thing an entrepreneur can do to affect it is to offer a good that the consumer considers of high(er) value or accept to sell it at a lower price. But the problem for the entrepreneur is that the asking price must also be high enough to cover the cost of production that was already incurred as well as the entrepreneur's profit requirement.

The entrepreneur's calculation is simple arithmetic, because the costs of production (inputs procured in the market) and the revenue of the final good offered for sale are both expressed in money prices. But when the decision is made to undertake the attempt to create new value, the price at which the final good can be sold is uncertain because it is based on two unknowns: the value of it to the consumer as well as their opportunity cost, which constitute the upper and lower bounds, respectively. (We briefly discussed this in Section 3.4 above.) The entrepreneur is thus left to his or her own ability to judge how much consumers may be willing to pay for the intended good in the market conditions that will then prevail.

The simple formula in the opening of the section establishes the necessary conditions for successful new value creation: the entrepreneur *and* the consumers gain. As the good has created new value, consumers have higher-valued goods to choose from, so they are better off than they were previously. If they were not made better off, they would not purchase the good. And as the good generated profits, the entrepreneur is also better off. For all parties involved, then, this is a gain. Or, to say the same thing with different words, the undertaking generates profits.

The issue that remains is to show how, given the uncertainty involved, this process can raise the standard of living. But let us first introduce additional complexity. We have until now abstracted from production stages.[18] But few, if any, production processes (individual production undertakings, as is the objective of most firms) span the distance, figuratively speaking, from original factors to consumption goods. This is especially the case, and increasingly so, in developed or advanced (specialized, high-value-producing) economies.

Most production processes use produced inputs (materials, tools, etc.) to produce their outputs. We relied on this fact in our discussion on the entrepreneurial firm above (see Section 3.3). Typically, they also rely on skilled labor, which means those employed have acquired relevant education and/or experience. Recognizing this fact does not change what we learned above but adds a layer of complexity that we need to address. This complexity also augments and therefore clarifies the extent of the problem that is sometimes referred to as *economic calculation* (Mises 1935, 1951; Hoff 1981).

In our previous discussion in Section 1.4, we referred to the consumer's valuation as the final arbiter of the value of every entrepreneur's production. Whereas the consumer still has this role as final arbiter of value in advanced economies, most entrepreneurs buy from and sell to other entrepreneurs within vast supply chains (e.g., Bylund 2015a, 2015b). For example, an iron mine produces iron ore that is sold as input to an iron smelting plant, which produces iron that is sold to a steel manufacturer, and so on; the steel may eventually be part of automobiles sold to consumers. Similarly, a farmer produces sugar beets that are sold to a processing plant to make sugar, which is then sold to a candy manufacturer, which supplies convenience stores with bagged candy to offer to consumers. In both of these examples, the inputs are refined as they travel through production stages to eventually end up in consumer goods offered to consumers.

In supply chains, therefore, the calculus becomes:

$$\text{value} > \text{price}_1 > \text{cost}_1/\text{price}_2 > \text{cost}_2 \ldots \text{price}_{(n-1)} > \text{cost}_{(n-1)}/\text{price}_n > \text{cost}_n$$

where n is the number of production stages within the supply chain. The question is, if we can derive the price of consumer goods from their (relative)

---

[18] We can conceptually conceive of market production as consisting of interdependent "stages," as did Menger (2007) and Böhm-Bawerk (1959), as a means for illustrating the point that entrepreneurial undertakings typically depend on market-provided inputs and many produce and sell outputs that are used as inputs in other production.

value to consumers, what is the basis for prices of intermediate goods that are exchanged between producers? It cannot be the value of the produced output, because consumers do not buy/consume intermediate goods. Intermediate goods do not have value in the sense that consumer goods do because they do not directly satisfy wants – they are means to produce other goods.

If all the production stages are carried out by the same producer, then they will have to wait longer for realized profits (or losses) but can still imagine the value of their produced good. But if different producers specialize in the different stages, which is generally accepted as a more productive state of affairs (e.g., Durkheim 1933; Smith 1976), then neither imagining nor waiting is an option. The iron smelting plant and sugar processor do not (and cannot) wait for consumer goods to be sold in order to figure out the price to charge the steel and candy manufacturers, respectively. They also cannot imagine how their respective outputs – steel and sugar – will be used, in what relative quantities, and how consumers will value the final goods produced. So, on what basis do they calculate whether their production may be a profitable undertaking?

To be useful, prices of intermediate goods should accurately, to the degree possible, represent economizing use of resources and intermediate goods. In other words, prices should represent the expected value contribution of stages of production. Mises explained the pricing process as continuous entrepreneurial bidding for inputs (Mises 1998, 332–33). This bidding takes place throughout the production structure with each entrepreneur (producer) attempting to secure inputs yet at the same time minimizing the cost of production in order to maintain (and increase) profitability. They will also adapt and adjust their production process, when necessary, to shift to alternative inputs if the structure of input prices change (Hayek 1945).

Entrepreneurs bid for resources guided by the prices they expect to receive for the goods produced, which set the ceiling for how much they can afford to pay for inputs. In other words, "price > cost" applies as a guide for all entrepreneurs throughout the production structure and in every supply chain. If prices of inputs (costs) increase across the board, such that production cannot be undertaken profitably with the expected output prices, and input prices are not expected to fall, then the entrepreneur will be forced to halt production and exit the market. If prices of inputs overall fall, entrepreneurs may increase production and expect higher profits to the extent prices of outputs will not fall as a result.

Those entrepreneurs who believe themselves able to produce the greatest value (and can convince owners of capital of the fact) will be able to afford the most productive resources. They can pay higher prices to make sure they acquire the preferred resources and will consequently bid up the prices so that the resources with highest-valued uses, per entrepreneurs' collective expectations, command the highest market prices. For some entrepreneurs, this bidding will make the resources they prefer too dear and thus they will consider options that may not be as technologically effective but are, given the relative prices, more cost effective. In this way, productive resources are put to their expected highest-valued uses.

We thus see that an advanced economy with numerous production stages largely functions the same way as our simplified models above. However, with the addition of entrepreneurial bidding for the means of production such that they determine the prices of resources based on their best assessment of their eventual value contributions.

This reinforces the point we have already made that *value* guides production but also establishes that it is entrepreneurs' expectations of value that determine the technology used in production processes. This undermines the common argument that technology is a matter of learning. Although the effectiveness of a specific technology used in production can certainly be learned, the *choice* of what technology to use is fundamentally economic. Relatively ineffective technologies may be economically preferable given the prices of inputs. Thus, knowledge of what would be more effective technology in the production of a certain type of good may not be considered actionable or even feasible depending on the expected value created and the value-based market prices of inputs. Technology, in other words, is a choice and a means in the entrepreneurial pursuit of value creation.

This process of determining factor prices through bidding and then choosing factors (and technology) based on those prices, driven by entrepreneurs' eagerness to earn profits yet moderated by their fear of suffering losses (Mises 2008), makes use of the collective judgment and imagination of entrepreneurs in a "division of intellectual labor" (Mises 1998, 705) to direct resources in the most economizing way. Given the nature of entrepreneurship, we cannot understand the market process without a proper understanding of economic calculation.

3.6 Economic Progress

What was stated in the previous section about pricing of original factors and intermediate goods throughout the production structure, and the adjustment made by entrepreneurs in response to changes (compare Hayek's (1945) tin example), is largely compatible with Model 1 and 2 but with the added complexity of production embedded in a market and thus occurring in conceptual stages of production. As entrepreneurs in these stages compete both horizontally and vertically (cf. Bylund 2016), prices and quantities should be expected to change over time. In Model 1, as errors are discovered and corrected, which causes entrepreneurs to adjust their resource allocations. In Model 2, as entrepreneurs respond to or act in anticipation of changing circumstances.

It is in this situation, with already determined market prices throughout the production structure, that innovative entrepreneurs enter to create new value. The calculus for them remains the same. However, the innovating entrepreneur judges the future differently and thus expects that their new value creation will provide value beyond what is already created and expected.

> the promoters, speculators, and entrepreneurs ... are the leaders on the way toward material progress. They are the first to understand that there is a discrepancy between what is done and what could be done. They guess what the consumers would like to have and are intent upon providing them with these things. (Mises 1998, 333)

Given our discussion in the previous sections, we can see how the greater value expectation allows innovative entrepreneurs to outbid other producers to thereby secure the needed inputs. They would also have greater chances of securing investment capital, if needed, as they can afford to pay higher interest rates on loans and because their higher expected return should be attractive to investors. Consequently, even if all productive resources would currently be tied up in existing production processes, the innovative entrepreneur could offer to pay resource owners a price that exceeds their current expected returns.

We thus find that there is no reason to conclude, as does Schumpeter, that entrepreneurship requires the extension of credit. It is not the case that "purchasing power does not flow towards him [the innovative entrepreneur] automatically, as to the producer in the circular flow, by the sale of what he produced in preceding periods" (Schumpeter 1934, 102). The innovative entrepreneur does not have revenue from sales to reinvest, but contrary to Schumpeter, purchasing power, in the form of productive investments and reinvestments, flows toward *value creation*.

The same argument applies whether the entrepreneur produces final goods for consumers or intermediate goods for other producers. However, those cases differ in one important respect: productive compatibility.

In an advanced market, production is vertically interdependent in such a way that the process (in stages) comprises a complete chain of operations between original factors and the consumer good. As a result, all stages must maintain compatibility with the preceding stage (or, for the first stage, original factors): they use (and must use because there are no alternatives) market-traded inputs, which they then transform into outputs. For all but the last stage – production of consumer goods – they must also produce outputs that are compatible with and thus can be used as inputs by the subsequent stage. In other words, the stages must interface with each other through standardized intermediate goods. However, this condition does not apply to the operations carried out within a stage, which are typically within a single business or production unit. Bylund writes:

> Market production is agnostic as to the execution of any particular stage, but depends on the intermediate goods, the stages' outputs, to be compatible through adhering to the established standard. This state of the production apparatus as specialised and standardised facilitates innovation since revolutionising production innovations can be adopted within a specific stage without affecting other stages (unless there is failure). (Bylund 2016, 79)

The creation of new consumer goods is open-ended in the sense that whatever goods are produced must provide the consumer with value to be feasible, but need not comply with specific requirements of subsequent producers (because there are none). The entrepreneur is therefore, technologically speaking, unrestricted with respect to what type of good can be created for consumers.

This is not the case for innovations that apply to other production stages, all of which must produce output that is compatible with the requirements of subsequent producers. This means innovations cannot be guided by value only, as is the case with new consumer goods, but must maintain the already established interfaces. In other words, the starting point – the inputs – is largely standardized and so is the end point – the output. Such innovations must therefore *increase productivity* to be viable.[19]

In the case of a new consumer good the entrepreneur expects to be able to charge a higher price than consumers are willing to pay for other goods. This expectation allows them to outbid competing entrepreneurs, and they can therefore secure inputs and earn profits. Their higher selling prices would be unlikely to persist, however, because they attract entrepreneurs seeking to capture part of the profits by emulating the original innovation and charging a more competitive (lower) price and also because the good may be disrupted by other entrepreneurs creating new (and even greater) value.

For productive innovations, in contrast, the price of the output must typically fall for the entrepreneur's undertaking to be viable. The reason for this is that producers in the subsequent stage expect to buy inputs that comply with a standard and select supplier primarily based on price (not value, as

---

[19] Bylund (2015a, 2016) argues that this is accomplished primarily by more intensive division of labor by replacing tasks with processes that more effectively produce the output.

consumers). Whereas there are situations where quality also plays a role, the innovating entrepreneur is still merely a supplier of inputs to the existing production process that comprises the subsequent stage – and therefore subject to its value-contributive capability. In other words, the focus of the innovator in intermediate stages of production must be to reimagine production in order to reduce the cost such that competitors can be outbid for the inputs, while the outputs can be sold at prices below the market price – and still offer a chance for profits. This would often be accomplished by establishing a production process that greatly reduces average cost at high production quantities. As with new consumer goods, the higher prices in the preceding stage signify higher returns that will attract entrepreneurs, who will then bid down the output prices.

In both cases, the effect is a higher standard of living: new consumer goods increase the value available to consumers and the productivity gains (reduced cost) from productive innovations increase the ability to produce at scale, which should lead to greater output quantity and thus ability to satisfy more consumer wants (which suggests lower prices).

It should also be noted that, just as in Model 3, we should expect more than one disruptive entrepreneur at a time. As they ultimately compete on and benefit from providing value to consumers, and their production undertakings are guided by the prices determined through value-based competitive bidding, the expected effect is a rising standard of living.

Simply put, market economies evolve and unfold – they *progress* – by means of entrepreneurship both within the production apparatus and in its end points: the consumer goods made available. The market process is directed by how entrepreneurs *en masse* expect to satisfy consumers, which determines market prices of original factors and intermediate goods based on the expected value output. As we saw in the previous section, these prices provide guidance to entrepreneurs for how best to economize in their productions.

Importantly, however, innovative entrepreneurs seek to produce in new ways or provide new goods valued higher by consumers such that they command higher market prices. This will, where successful, generate profits from the increased value creation. For intermediate goods, profits are due to *increased productivity*, which allows the entrepreneur to bid over competitors for inputs and bid under for outputs while keeping the per-unit cost of production lower than the market standard. For consumer goods, profits are generated from the greater difference between the selling prices for the new good and market input prices determined by entrepreneurs' value-based bidding, that is, the additional *value created*. Combined, these two contributions facilitate increased quantity of and more valuable goods available for consumers, whose standard of living thus increases.

4 Political Economy

Economic action and, importantly, entrepreneurship take place within, react on, and cause change to the economy, which therefore evolves and unfolds over time. Due to the value-creative aim and effect of entrepreneurship, the market *progresses* and is best understood as a *process*.

This does not mean that it is without limitations and constraints, however. Such limitations exist in primarily two forms, which will be discussed in this section. The first is the economy's real constraints due to insufficient availability of productive resources to satisfy all wants at once. The impact of this constraint – that is, scarcity – is lessened and reduced by successful entrepreneurship, which increases value production within and despite the physical limits of the world.

The other is human-made limitations that are imposed on or otherwise influence or direct economic action. These limitations, often in the form of norms or rules, comprise the institutional environment, which can streamline and facilitate as well as restrict and thwart entrepreneurship and production.

We will discuss both of these in order, then elaborate on the positive and negative effects of institutions on the market process.

4.1 Resources and Performance

As the market process is not directed toward the maximum value output of the existing production structure, as many equilibrium models assume, but by entrepreneurs' new value creation, efficiency in resource use is an inappropriate yardstick for the performance of the market process. Schumpeter thus concludes that "there is no point in appraising the performance of that process *ex visu* of a given point of time; we must judge its performance over time, as it unfolds through decades or centuries" (1947, 83). Indeed, as entrepreneurs find new and better ways of serving consumers – as they innovate – they also disrupt and replace production structures already in place. Progress, in other words, is not a matter of putting all resources to use in production but to figure out better ways of creating value.

Yet the common assumption in economic analysis is the comparatively static "allocative efficiency" view of the economy, what we above captured in Model 1 and 2 – not the entrepreneurial market process.[20] This static perspective, which we showed is not a relevant model for the real market, suggests that any "slack" (currently unused or "idle" productive resources (Hutt 1939)) in the economy implies a lower level of production than is possible given resources

---

[20] Macroeconomic theory and policy tend to be based on this thesis, which often fails to properly account for entrepreneurship (Bylund 2016b).

available. The "idle" resources doctrine, as it is sometimes called, thus concludes that the economy could produce more value if all resources were put into present use. Whenever it does not, we are suffering a "market failure," meaning the market's allocation of resources is not Pareto optimal. It would then appear to follow that it may be beneficial to task the government with spending to stimulate increased use of "idle" resources.

However, following out process perspective, and as Hutt (1939) shows, many resources that may be perceived as "idle" to an observer are actually already committed to production. For example, a piece of apparently unused land may be part of a project to create new infrastructure, a road or a factory, intended to play an important role in production processes for years to come. Putting that piece of land into immediate use may thwart its intended (higher-valued) use.

In other cases, some period of "idleness" may be advantageous in value production terms to putting the resource to immediate new use. This would be the case with, for example, an engineer seeking employment as engineer (highly productive), while there are unfilled positions for manual labor (relatively less productive). Total value output could in fact *increase* if the engineer is not immediately put to work as manual labor but instead is afforded the "idle" time to find more productive employment (Hutt 1939). Similarly, an entrepreneur in the process of establishing production of an anticipated new value may not yet have acquired all resources necessary or has yet to start production. It would be false to assume that the entrepreneur's resources are idle or that they are underutilized.

Schumpeter goes further and suggests that there may be value in having slack in the economy because those idle resources, even if they are truly idle, are therefore available for entrepreneurs seeking to create new value. This, in turn, may be a prerequisite for creating new combinations that bring about economic development:

> A system – any system, economic or other – that at *every* given point of time fully utilizes its possibilities to the best advantage may yet in the long run be inferior to a system that does so at *no* given point in time, because the latter's failure to do so may be a condition for the level or speed of long-run performance. (Schumpeter 1947, 83, emphasis in original)

Our previous discussion seems to offer some support for this view. We found that an entrepreneurial market process should outperform a static system in terms of value output despite not maximizing the present use of every resource. However, unlike Schumpeter we found that the process may not require slack or expanded credit to progress – it requires only entrepreneurial imagination that new value creation is possible. Based on the imagined value creation, entrepreneurs can justify bidding higher for needed factors than competing entrepreneurs.[21]

The obverse is also not true: entrepreneurship cannot guarantee that resources that are used in production will therefore create value. Many entrepreneurial undertakings fail. This includes undertakings that satisfy a market need and does so effectively. For example, we can imagine that producers of horse carriages and buggy whips were highly effective or even maximized their resource usage before Ford introduced the Model T. Their "maximizing" means nothing as the new value offered by Ford greatly surpassed the value of producing buggy whips, thus effecting what Schumpeter called "creative destruction."

In other words, there is no obvious correlation between resource utilization and value creation. That there are idle resources in an economy does not indicate lacking, less-than-maximized value creation. Similarly, full resource utilization – for example, full employment – does not indicate that an economy is maximizing its value output.[22]

4.2 Institutional Environment

In addition to the real constraints, there are human-generated extra-economic forces in play too – institutions. They shape the outcome of the market process although they do not therefore change the nature of economic forces (which our Models 1, 2, and 3 captured). As Ronald H. Coase noted, "It makes little sense for economists to discuss the process of exchange without specifying the institutional setting within which the trading takes place, since this affects the incentives to produce and the costs of transacting" (Coase 1992, 718).

As is now commonly recognized, the institutional environment affects entrepreneurship – which projects are, will, and can be undertaken – and entrepreneurial outcomes as well. Thus, the quality of institutions can affect to what degree entrepreneurship is productive (value-creative, as discussed primarily in Section 3.2), unproductive (redistributive), and destructive (benefitting the entrepreneur at the expense of society overall) (Baumol 1990; Sobel 2008).

---

[21] Schumpeter appears to refer to the entrepreneur's access to the money necessary to purchase resources already in use, but this is a separate issue that has to do with the overall functioning of the financial system, the entrepreneur's own wealth, or the ability to persuade lenders to provide financing. For our purposes, the fact that the imagined value justifies paying higher prices for resources is sufficient to indicate access to productive capital.

[22] This suggests a reason for why the paradox of plenty (or the resource curse), which states that countries with an abundance of natural resources tend to have lower economic growth rates and less economic development than countries with less resources (e.g., Sachs and Warner 1999), applies. Access to (physical) resources has no obvious, if any, relationship with value created.

Institutions are here understood as the "humanly devised constraints that shape human interaction" (North 1990, 3). They provide the "rules of the game" that together with the laws of economics determine the "play of the game." Consequently, Douglass C. North finds:

> Throughout history, institutions have been devised by human beings to create order and reduce uncertainty in exchange. Together with the standard constraints of economics they define the choice set and therefore determine transaction and production costs and hence the profitability and feasibility of engaging in economic activity. They evolve incrementally, connecting the past with the present and the future; history in consequence is largely a story of institutional evolution. (North 1991, 97)

However, whereas institutions reduce uncertainty by incentivizing conformity in action, the institutional environment also interacts with entrepreneurship in dynamic ways (Boettke and Coyne 2009). Recent research has increasingly acknowledged that the relationship between institutions and entrepreneurship is complex and bidirectional (Elert and Henrekson 2017): institutions affect entrepreneurship but entrepreneurship also effects change on institutions.

This dynamic was observed decades ago:

> Entrepreneurs (whether ancient or modern) work within an institutional environment that itself often yields to entrepreneurial efforts. That is to say, there are "political entrepreneurs" who expend efforts to change institutional structures and practices in order to benefit themselves. (Hébert and Link 2009, 4; cf. 1988, 1989)

But there is more to this than the entrepreneur's binary choice between complying with existing rules (regulations, standards, etc.) and using political clout to gain favors (Holcombe 2018). Oliver E. Williamson (2000) suggests that the institutional environment comprises a system of conceptual layers. While institutions "evolve incrementally," as North observes, they also exist in a hierarchical system with an internal dynamic. This system and its components, both its layers and specific institutions, interact with, affect, and are affected by economic practice.

In Williamson's model, the top level (L1) consists of informal institutions that are slow to change (values, norms, etc.), whereas the second (L2) comprises the formal institutions that primarily are provided by the government in the form of laws, regulations, and compulsory standards. Imposing and enforcing rules under L2 that contradict the informal institutions of L1 creates tension and uncertainty for actors, which could therefore undermine the legitimacy of L2. There is thus a cost advantage in institutional alignment and, as a result, a natural tendency for institutions to be aligned.

Whereas L1 and L2 provide the framework for economic organizing and action, the lower levels L3 (governance structures) and L4 (market exchange, prices) constitute the standards of economic practice. This is where production is organized, and resources allocated toward productive ends. As with L1 and L2, institutions on each level impose constraints on the lower levels by changing the cost structure such that aligned action is relatively less costly. For example, long-term contracting or the creation of formal organizations on L3 imposes constraints on resource allocations in L4.

The cost structure of an institutional environment facilitates economizing, which means there are cost reasons for institutions on different levels to become aligned and therefore provide actors and actions with a uniform, noncontradictory set of expectations. But they are not always aligned. For example, a long-term contract can require a resource allocation that imposes a loss on one or more of the parties as market prices change. This cost implies an incentive to renege, which causes uncertainty as the parties may not be able to trust each other to comply with the terms of the contract. Similarly, a society's norms and values (L1) can be at odds with what is mandated by laws and regulations (L2), a misalignment that suggests that consumers and policymakers have different and perhaps conflicting expectations on producers. In such cases, the institutions do not provide guidance for economic actions but, on the contrary, impose additional costs due to institutional uncertainty (Bylund and McCaffrey 2017).

However, whereas most entrepreneurship takes place within the overall institutional environment, it is not merely subject to the rules and standards that institutions impose. On the contrary, entrepreneurs can and do choose strategies with respect to the institutional environment or specific institutions deemed of particular importance. The literature identifies four such strategies: abiding entrepreneurship, which complies with existing institutional rules; evasive entrepreneurship, which seeks to avoid the constraints of some or all institutions (Elert and Henrekson 2016); altering entrepreneurship, which seeks to impose change to the institutional environment (McCaffrey and Salerno 2011); and exit, which may be the only appropriate action when institutional impositions become too burdensome (Bylund and McCaffrey 2017).

But there are also places and situations where there is a lack of institutions or institutional support, which can thwart entrepreneurship and other economic actions. In such "institutional voids" entrepreneurs must bear the uncertainty of acting without guidance from institutions. Common examples of this include developing or transition economies and countries with corrupt governments, but this is also the case for informal or "black market" entrepreneurship (e.g., Webb et al. 2009). This suggests that there may be an additional entrepreneurial strategy: to create one's own institutions, which can be designed to solve specific issues that the present institutional environment does not effectively address.

Furthermore, our discussion on entrepreneurial disruption suggests that entrepreneurs can, through their value-creative innovations, create or give rise to new institutional voids as they establish production beyond the production possibilities frontier and therefore break new economic ground. Whereas institutions provide the general framework of rules for economic action, previously unrealized and unforeseen innovations can create situations beyond what existing institutions properly regulate. Due to institutional inertia, those situations may not have institutionally supported solutions.

It is easy to presume that institutions must be designed and imposed top-down, but history shows that this is not necessarily the case. In fact, institutions on Williamson's top level are not designed or even limited by designed rules. Institutional rules can also emerge as standards or orders out of the actions and interactions of entrepreneurs – "the result of human action, but not the execution of any human design" in Ferguson's (1782, 205) now-famous phrase. This type of phenomenon, so-called "spontaneous orders," may be much more prevalent than is often recognized. The price mechanism is one such order, which in markets determines prices through entrepreneurial bidding.

Entrepreneurial pursuits of value creation can and do bring about institutional orders, whether of local or global impact, that are largely unintended and undesigned.

4.3 Institutions as Facilitators

There is a vast body of research that substantiates the claim that high-quality institutions, and in particular economic freedom, correlate with or is even a prerequisite for a higher standard of living. For example, indices of economic freedom, such as the Fraser Institute's Economic Freedom of the World (Gwartney, Lawson, and Murphy 2023) and the Heritage Foundation's Index of Economic Freedom (Kim 2023), show strong correlations between how economically free and wealthy nations are. There is also a historical relationship between well-functioning institutions and economic performance (North 1990, 1994; Davis and North 1971). Rich countries tend to have circumscribed political power, which implies fewer and lesser burdens imposed on economic activity, whereas poor countries often suffer from extractive institutions (Acemoglu and Robinson 2008, 2012).

As the driving force of the economy, entrepreneurship is and has long been core to explaining economic growth (e.g., Say 1836; Schumpeter 1934). Recent research has corroborated that there is such a relationship or even that entrepreneurship *causes* economic growth (e.g., Wennekers and Thurik 1999; Audretsch, Keilbach, and Lehmann 2006). We developed a theoretical argument for why this is so in previous sections (see in particular Section 3.6).

Entrepreneurship should therefore also be key to understanding how economic freedom, which precedes and provides context for entrepreneurial action, translates into economic growth and prosperity. That there is a link has been established in various research (see Bylund, Klein, and McCaffrey 2024 for a recent overview) and has recently regained scholarly attention in the study of institutional entrepreneurship (e.g., Henrekson and Sanandaji 2011) as we saw in Section 4.2. Randall G. Holcombe notes:

> If entrepreneurship is the key to economic progress, and if economies can be made more entrepreneurial, an important policy issue is how entrepreneurship can be encouraged. The answer is that institutions that create economic freedom by protecting property rights and removing impediments to market exchange encourage entrepreneurship and lead to economic progress. (Holcombe 2007, 112)

The indices already mentioned include in their measures of economic freedom a country's protection of property rights, the rule of law, and size of government, thereby accounting for the institutional environment. The quality of institutions (e.g., Chowdhury, Audretsch, and Belitski 2019) and their stability (e.g., Higgs 1997; Bennett, Boudreaux, and Nikolaev 2023) have been found to be important to facilitate productive entrepreneurship. Others have found that the institutional burden on entrepreneurship also plays an important role in determining the nature, frequency, and outcomes of entrepreneurship (e.g., De Soto 2000; D'Andrea 2023). This research suggests that the greater quality and stability, and the lesser the burden, of the institutional environment, the greater the quantity and quality of entrepreneurship.

Institutions could do more than passively facilitate entrepreneurship, however. They could potentially be designed to incentivize and actively support entrepreneurship to thereby increase quantity and, perhaps, quality. In contrast to the idle resources doctrine, using policy to augment and enable entrepreneurship would strengthen the market's own mechanisms for value creation and therefore could create societal benefit – higher standard of living and, probably, increased employment. Such efforts have largely been disappointing, however. Lerner (2009) documents how there certainly are hubs of entrepreneurial activity following government investments, but also that there are many failed efforts that have generated enormous waste of public funds. Overall, it is difficult to make a case for the "entrepreneurial state" (Mazzucato 2011; cf. Mingardi 2015) – public policies directly supporting entrepreneurship in order to augment economic progress – both in theory and practice (Wennberg and Sandström 2022).

Similarly for so-called publicly funded "moonshot" projects, which are massive government investments such as the US Space Program that generate spin-off innovations and increase economic activity by creating opportunities for suppliers. Some argue that these projects do not only create net value for society, but that they should be used by policymakers to direct the economy (Mazzucato 2018). However, research finds that it is questionable if such projects generate more economic growth and value than the entrepreneurship they crowd out – and that would otherwise take place elsewhere in the economy (Audretsch and Fiedler 2023; Henrekson, Sandström, and Stenkula 2024).

From our new value creation perspective, these conclusions are not surprising. Entrepreneurs are ultimately incentivized by earning profits, which, under economic freedom and a generally supportive institutional environment, are the result of contributing value to consumers in a cost-effective way. The process is endogenously disruptive as innovative entrepreneurs seek to outdo the value creative efforts of other entrepreneurs by providing consumers with new, previously unseen value. Any restrictions imposed on this behavior, whether or not institutional, should therefore mean less value output than otherwise and, as a result, comparatively *lower* standard of living (we will discuss this in the next section).

The same result should be expected from active public investments, incentives, and other direct support aimed to increase entrepreneurship in a specific area, industry, or technology. Whereas the support will attract entrepreneurs, it also shifts entrepreneurial returns away from innovations where consumers would have preferred them (and thus provided higher profits from capturing part of the value created) to where they instead please policymakers or experts.[23] Public investments may facilitate achieving political goals, but ultimately shifts entrepreneurial value-creation efforts away from where they would be expected – by entrepreneurs themselves – to create most value.

Given the theory we have developed and extant research on entrepreneurship-driven economic growth, we should expect the institutional environment most conducive to value-creative entrepreneurship to be one that neither restricts nor distorts it but reduces uncertainty for entrepreneurial undertakings – including innovative entrepreneurship. In other words, an aligned institutional structure that improves predictability but does not impose restrictions on value-creation.

---

[23] We are here leaving out the possibility of expert failure, which may be more common than often recognized (Koppl 2018).

4.4 Institutions as Impediments

The institutional environment is not only supportive but can also impede entrepreneurship. Such stifling effects are the result of imposing costs on entrepreneurs, which they would otherwise not need to bear. As a result, entrepreneurship may be undertaken at an overall lower quantity in the economy, or entrepreneurial undertakings may be distorted such that they create suboptimal or unwanted outcomes. We will here elaborate on the respective effects of institutional uncertainty, which imposes institution-based costs on entrepreneurs that change their behavior, regulations, which restrict the scope of entrepreneurial opportunities in the economy, and other types of bureaucratic burdens imposed on entrepreneurial action.

Institutional uncertainty arises "when entrepreneurs anticipate misalignments, incongruences, or contradictions between institutions on different levels" (Bylund and McCaffrey 2017, 462). For example, Higgs (1997) argues that an important reason the Great Depression lasted for so long was a mismatch between political rhetoric and practice: the New Deal imposed costs on business, but the anti-business rhetoric from political decision-makers went much further and raised questions about whether policymakers would allow the capitalist system to remain intact. This caused "regime uncertainty," a special case of institutional uncertainty.

As a result, entrepreneurs and private investors in the 1930s faced not only the regular uncertainty of the market, which they are largely equipped or prepared to bear, but also the uncertainty of whether there would be a system change. Specifically, the rhetoric suggested to them that private business and property rights protections may soon be greatly circumscribed or even abolished. This made, per Higgs, investors hesitant to act as they otherwise would have. After all, why make investments for profit if you cannot trust that you will remain the owner of the property and that the profits will accrue to you?

Such institutional uncertainty thus may cause entrepreneurs to adopt strategies with respect to the institutional environment that they otherwise would not have chosen.

> Institutional uncertainty changes entrepreneurs' relative costs of bearing uncertainty in their typical abiding activities. When these costs are high, entrepreneurs have little choice but to evade institutions, alter them through action at a different institutional level, or exit the market. (Bylund and McCaffrey 2017, 462)

Another example adjacent to institutional uncertainty is captured by the Austrian theory of the business cycle (ABCT; see e.g., Mises 1953; Salerno 2012). Here the signals on which entrepreneurs rely have been distorted such that entrepreneurs are misled to make investments they otherwise would not have made. In ABCT, it is banks' extension of credit that forces down the market interest rate below the level it would otherwise have been (the "natural" rate; Wicksell 1936). As a result, it becomes cheaper to borrow, which makes more entrepreneurial investments appear profitable. Also, the lower rate makes projects with more distant future returns seem more profitable because their present value is higher.[24]

The lower interest rate may therefore increase the quantity of entrepreneurship as more entrepreneurs find it worthwhile to try their "luck." There will as a result be more (and riskier) investments than the economy otherwise would have suggested feasible. The failure rate of these undertakings should for this reason be expected higher than usual. It will also distort the structure of entrepreneurship as entrepreneurs are incentivized to invest more in projects with temporally distant returns. Consequently, there will be relative overinvestment in such projects and relative underinvestment in others, that is, malinvestments.

We do not need to analyze in detail the processes and mechanisms of ABCT[25] to see how a distorted signal – the lower interest rate – makes entrepreneurs and potential entrepreneurs behave differently. Some entrepreneurs may realize that the interest rate is artificially low, but their incentive is still to take advantage of the lower cost of capital by starting new businesses and scaling up existing ones. Although the boom will conclude with a bust, even if entrepreneurs recognize this, they will also see that there is money to be made in the boom phase.

Regulations are restrictions imposed on the economy by an external party, typically the government or a government agency. The regulations we are here interested in are imposed to change economic practice or outcomes by legally restricting entrepreneurs' behavior – what they can do and how. Whereas they are imposed with the intention to cause specific expected effects, regulations often also have unintended consequences. Some regulations are also ineffective in the sense that they that do not effect change on observable economic behavior in the present or near future (such as a law that imposes a minimum wage below what is the current market wage) (Bylund 2016a).

Our perspective here makes the outcome of regulations on entrepreneurial action clear. A restriction imposed on entrepreneurship, whether or not for good

---

[24] Present value is the future returns discounted using the interest rate. For example, the present value of $10,000 a year from now is $9,000 at an interest rate of 10 percent per annum, whereas it is $9,500 at 5 percent.

[25] There is a large literature available on ABCT and applications of the theory. For a simple overview, see Bylund (2022b, ch. 8), and for an application on the Great Depression, see Rothbard (2000).

reason, will cause entrepreneurs to not pursue value creation undertakings that will be burdened by the regulation – at least not to the extent they otherwise would have. This means that consumers will not receive the potential value the entrepreneurs would have created, but also that the entrepreneurs may instead choose to pursue opportunities elsewhere. In other words, regulations typically cause a shift in entrepreneurial activity from activities where the restriction applies to where it does not (or applies to a lesser extent). Whereas regulations intend the former, a restriction of entrepreneurial activity with respect to some market, method, or good, the nature and extent of the latter – what entrepreneurs do instead – depends on how, when, and where entrepreneurs imagine they can create value. As entrepreneurial imagination is difficult, if not impossible, to predict, all regulations have some degree of unintended consequences.

Importantly, the implication is also that entrepreneurs pursue value creations of expected lower value than otherwise would have been the case. If this were not the case, they would have chosen those opportunities without the regulation, and it would therefore not have caused a shift.

Also, we find using our value-creation perspective that many of the regulations that do not have a direct effect on entrepreneurs can still constrain entrepreneurship. Innovative entrepreneurship is directed by what value entrepreneurs imagine that they can provide for consumers, which means regulations that do not seem to have an effect on economic behavior in the observable present may still restrict potential entrepreneurs from pursuing new value creation in the future.

We cannot predict what potential future entrepreneurs might imagine that they can do for consumers and therefore we cannot predict the extent to which a regulation, whether or not it has directly observable effects, may affect entrepreneurial value creation. In fact, much of the cost in terms of *unrealized value creation* therefore remains unaccounted for in economic analyses of regulations (Bylund 2016a). The effect of regulations, as Bylund (2022b, 129) notes, is that "[t]he economy is on an overall lower-value trajectory, which means the loss [due to regulations] is all the value that would have otherwise been attained."

Finally, *bureaucratic burden* refers to "red tape" impositions that, in addition to regulations as already discussed, increase the difficulty, cost, or time commitment for entrepreneurs to do entrepreneurship "by the book" – to be compliant with and thus act in accordance with existing laws, rules, and other requirements. Such burdens may be imposed as a means for enforcing regulations already in place or to further control some outcome deemed preferable (such as quality of good, worker health and safety, environmental impact). They include compliance issues and zoning, licensing and reporting requirements, etc.

Naturally, any increased cost due to bureaucratic burdens makes the opportunity less beneficial in money terms. But the real impact can be different than the estimated effect on the entrepreneur's expected profits. Entrepreneurs do not maximize profits, which we found in previous sections to be impossible. They pursue what they imagine will be of value to consumers *on the consumers' terms* and hope to capture some of this value by charging a price in excess of production costs.

A common but often by economic theorists overlooked reason for people to start their own business is autonomy, a sense of freedom in one's profession and career. Different burdens can thus have different effects based on how those burdens are perceived by entrepreneurs (Packard and Bylund 2021; see also Bylund and Packard 2022). For example, entrepreneurs may disproportionally discount opportunities that require governmental or third-party insight into their operations (Wood, Bylund, and Bradley 2016).

5 Concluding Remarks

This Element attempted to prove the importance of including entrepreneurship in the analysis of economics beyond what is done in Evolutionary Economics. There is much more to this than "simply" addressing the issue of economic growth. In fact, as we argued in Section 2, incorporating entrepreneurship as imaginative value creation in our conception of the market economy fundamentally alters our understanding of how the economy works. The entrepreneurial economy is a process in constant movement, not a static system; it is dynamic and unfolding, not merely responsive; and it harbors both disruptive and spasmodic change, not an even flow. In other words, an entrepreneurial economy *evolves*. The driving force of this evolution is the entrepreneur.

The entrepreneur and entrepreneurship play central roles in the history of economic thought. For example, and as we noted in Section 1.1, Richard Cantillon theorized on entrepreneurship as uncertainty-bearing in the early 18th century, some half-century before Adam Smith published his well-known tome *An Inquiry into the Nature and Causes of the Wealth of Nations* in 1776. And the French economist Jean-Baptiste Say famously studied entrepreneurs as organizers and leaders of an economy. Indeed, theorizing on the evolution of and value creation in an economy starts with and requires that we theorize on the entrepreneur. This should be unsurprising, since the size, evolution, and effectiveness of the totality of society's production undertakings that seek to lessen the burden of scarcity – the economy – are all caused by entrepreneurship.

Yet we still know very little about this phenomenon beyond the person and apparent correlations in aggregate statistics. The former, drawing from psychology, stresses the person's entrepreneurial mindset, including their propensity to take on risk, to see things differently, to go against the grain, and value autonomy, all of which can be both good and bad. The latter, which is the approach in macroeconomics, refers to how the number of startups and small businesses or people who are self-employed relate to, for example, the rate of increase in the gross domestic product (GDP), (un)employment rates, and so on. But neither captures the impact of the entrepreneurship function on the economy's production structure, its evolution over time, or its capacity to generate prosperity in society.

As a result, we are still quite far from an advanced understanding of the economy as an entrepreneurially driven process directed by (imagined and anticipated) value creation. Entrepreneurship studies enlightens us about the how, what, and why of entrepreneurship on the individual or firm level. Economics provides powerful models for recognizing outcomes and assessing effects of policy on the level of the industry or economy. But the levels are not independent or separate but interdependent and mutually constituting. If we are to understand the economy as it really is and how it works, we must recognize and explain its causalities, interactions, interdependencies, and patterns – and how, why, and by what means they evolve over time. To accomplish this, we must do more than recognize the importance of entrepreneurship. We must place entrepreneurship at the very center of what makes, shapes, and defines an economy. To do so indeed requires "a major reconstruction of the theoretical foundations of our discipline" (Nelson and Winter 1982, 4).

This Element constitutes an early attempt at such a reconstruction by specifying both the function of entrepreneurship and how it alters our conceptions of the market as an evolutionary process. We found that Evolutionary Economics certainly takes important steps in this direction but that it falls short of the full explanation. Our focus on value creation allowed us to elaborate on the impact and implications of entrepreneurship, which ultimately reverses the causality of economic action: it is not simply that economic production creates value, but that entrepreneurial expectations (or, if you will, their judgments and imaginations) of future value that justifies and, in this sense, causes production.

A value-directed market is not and cannot be a matter of knowledge because future market conditions are always unknown; knowledge is a result and outcome of economic production but not an explanation for it. Technology and technological knowledge facilitate production and may inspire entrepreneurial imagination by indicating what may be possible but do not explain innovation or even determine the technology chosen for implementing it. Entrepreneurs do this, guided by their expectations of serving consumers.

References

Acemoglu, Daron, and James A. Robinson. 2008. *The Role of Institutions in Growth and Development*. Vol. 10. Washington, DC: World Bank.

———. 2012. *Why Nations Fail: The Origins of Power, Prosperity, and Poverty*. New York: Crown Books.

Acs, Zoltan J. 1992. "Small Business Economics: A Global Perspective." *Challenge* 35 (6): 38–44.

Alvarez, Sharon A., and Jay B. Barney. 2007. "Discovery and Creation: Alternative Theories of Entrepreneurial Action." *Strategic Entrepreneurship Journal* 1 (1–2): 11–26.

Audretsch, David B., and Antje Fiedler. 2023. "Does the Entrepreneurial State Crowd out Entrepreneurship?" *Small Business Economics* 60 (2): 573–89.

Audretsch, David B., Max C. Keilbach, and Erik E. Lehmann. 2006. *Entrepreneurship and Economic Growth*. Oxford: Oxford University Press.

Barringer, Bruce R., and R. Duane Ireland. 2019. *Successfully Launching New Ventures*. New York: Pearson.

Baumol, William J. 1968. "Entrepreneurship in Economic Theory." *The American Economic Review* 58 (2): 64–71.

———. 1990. "Entrepreneurship: Productive, Unproductive, and Destructive." *Journal of Political Economy* 98: 893–919.

———. 1993. "Formal Entrepreneurship Theory in Economics: Existence and Bounds." *Journal of Business Venturing* 8 (3): 197–210.

Bennett, Daniel L., Christopher Boudreaux, and Boris Nikolaev. 2023. "Populist Discourse and Entrepreneurship: The Role of Political Ideology and Institutions." *Journal of International Business Studies* 54 (1): 151–81.

Blaug, Mark. 2003. "The Formalist Revolution of the 1950s." *Journal of the History of Economic Thought* 25 (2): 145–56.

Boettke, Peter J., and Christopher J. Coyne. 2009. *Context Matters: Institutions and Entrepreneurship*. Vol. 22. Now Publishers.

Böhm-Bawerk, Eugen von. 1959. *Positive Theory of Capital*. Vol. 2. Capital and Interest. South Holland, IL: Libertarian Press.

Bower, Joseph L., and Clayton M. Christensen. 1995. "Disruptive Technologies: Catching the Wave." *Harvard Business Review* 73 (1): 43–53.

Brock, William A., and David S. Evans. 1989. "Small Business Economics." *Small Business Economics* 1: 7–20.

Brown, Christopher, and Mark Thornton. 2013. "How Entrepreneurship Theory Created Economics." *Quarterly Journal of Austrian Economics* 16 (4): 401–20.

Buenstorf, Guido. 2007. "Creation and Pursuit of Entrepreneurial Opportunities: An Evolutionary Economics Perspective." *Small Business Economics* 28: 323–37.

Bylund, Per L. 2011. "Division of Labor and the Firm: An Austrian Attempt at Explaining the Firm in the Market." *Quarterly Journal of Austrian Economics* 14 (2): 188–215.

2015a. "Explaining Firm Emergence: Specialization, Transaction Costs, and the Integration Process." *Managerial & Decision Economics* 36 (4): 221–38.

2015b. "Signifying Williamson's Contribution to the Transaction Cost Approach: An Agent-Based Simulation of Coasean Transaction Costs and Specialization." *Journal of Management Studies* 52 (1): 148–74.

2015d. "The Realm of Entrepreneurship in the Market: Capital Theory, Production, and Change." In *The Next Generation of Austrian Economics: Essays in Honor of Joseph T. Salerno*, edited by Per L. Bylund and David Howden, 89–104. Auburn, AL: Ludwig von Mises Institute.

2016. *The Problem of Production: A New Theory of the Firm*. London: Routledge.

2016a. *The Seen, the Unseen, and the Unrealized: How Regulations Affect Our Everyday Lives*. Lanham: Lexington Books.

2016b. "What the Entrepreneurial Problem Reveals about Keynesian Macroeconomics." In *What's Wrong with Keynesian Economic Theory?*, edited by Steven Kates, 26–43. Cheltenham: Edward Elgar.

2018. "Management Is What's Wrong with Socialism: Cost at the Expense of Value." In *The Economic Theory of Costs: Foundations and New Directions*, edited by Matthew McCaffrey, 225–41. Abingdon: Routledge.

2019. "Entrepreneurship, Uncertainty, and Judgment: A Model for Understanding the Uncertainty Borne by Entrepreneurs."

2020. "Finding the Entrepreneur-Promoter: A Praxeological Inquiry." *Quarterly Journal of Austrian Economics* 23 (3–4): 355–89.

2021. "The Firm versus the Market: Dehomogenizing the Transaction Cost Theories of Coase and Williamson." *Strategic Management Review* 2 (1): 79–118. https://doi.org/10.1561/111.00000018.

2022a. "Entrepreneurship and the Market Process." In *A Modern Guide to Austrian Economics*, edited by Per L. Bylund, 84–102. Cheltenham: Edward Elgar.

2022b. *How to Think about the Economy: A Primer*. Auburn, AL: Ludwig von Mises Institute.

2024. "Beyond Dynamic Efficiency: Entrepreneurship and the Progressing Economy." *Cosmos + Taxis* 12 (11+12): 107–16.

Bylund, Per L., and Matthew McCaffrey. 2017. "A Theory of Entrepreneurship and Institutional Uncertainty." *Journal of Business Venturing* 32 (5): 461–75.

Bylund, Per L., and Mark D. Packard. 2022. "Subjective Value in Entrepreneurship." *Small Business Economics* 58 (3): 1243–60. https://doi.org/10.1007/s11187-021-00451-2.

Bylund, Per L., Peter G. Klein, and Matthew McCaffrey. 2024. "Entrepreneurship and Economic Freedom." In *Handbook of Research on Economic Freedom*, edited by Niclas Berggren, 242–58. Cheltenham: Edward Elgar.

Cantillon, Richard. 1931. *Essai Sur La Nature Du Commerce En Général*. Translated by C. B. Henry Higgs. London: Macmillan.

Carree, Martin A., and A. Roy Thurik. 2010. "The Impact of Entrepreneurship on Economic Growth." In *Handbook of Entrepreneurship Research*, edited by Zoltan J. Acs and David B. Audretsch, 5: 557–94. International Handbook Series on Entrepreneurship. New York: Springer.

Chowdhury, Farzana, David B. Audretsch, and Maksim Belitski. 2019. "Institutions and Entrepreneurship Quality." *Entrepreneurship Theory and Practice* 43 (1): 51–81.

Christensen, Clayton M., Michael E. Raynor, and Rory McDonald. 2015. "What Is Disruptive Innovation?" *Harvard Business Review*, no. December.

Coase, Ronald H. 1937. "The Nature of the Firm." *Economica* 4 (16): 386–405.

1960. "The Problem of Social Cost." *Journal of Law and Economics* 3 (1): 1–44.

1992. "The Institutional Structure of Production." *The American Economic Review* 82 (4): 713–19.

D'Andrea, Fernando Antonio Monteiro Christoph. 2023. "Entrepreneurship and Institutional Uncertainty." *Journal of Entrepreneurship and Public Policy* 12 (1): 10–31. https://doi.org/10.1108/JEPP-01-2022-0018.

Davis, Lance E., and Douglass C. North. 1971. *Institutional Change and American Economic Growth*. New York: Cambridge University Press.

De Soto, Hernando. 2000. *The Mystery of Capital: Why Capitalism Triumphs in the West and Fails Everywhere Else*. New York: Basic Books.

Demsetz, Harold. 1983. "The Neglect of the Entrepreneur." In *Entrepreneurship*, edited by Joshua Ronen, 271–80. Lexington: Lexington Press.

2011. "R. H. Coase and the Neoclassical Model of the Economic System." *Journal of Law and Economics* 54 (4): S7–S13.

Dopfer, Kurt. 2005. "Evolutionary Economics: A Theoretical Framework." In *The Evolutionary Foundations of Economics*, edited by Kurt Dopfer, 3–55. Cambridge: Cambridge University Press.

Durkheim, Emile. 1933. *The Division of Labor in Society*. New York: The Free Press.

Elert, Niklas, and Magnus Henrekson. 2016. "Evasive Entrepreneurship." *Small Business Economics* 47 (1): 95–113.

——— 2017. "Entrepreneurship and Institutions: A Bidirectional Relationship." *Foundations and Trends® in Entrepreneurship* 13 (3): 191–263.

Ferguson, Adam. 1782. *An Essay on the History of Civil Society*. London: T. Cadell.

Friedman, Milton. 1953. "The Methodology of Positive Economics." In *Essays in Positive Economics*, 3–43. Chicago: University of Chicago Press.

Gartner, William B. 2007. "Entrepreneurial Narrative and a Science of the Imagination." *Journal of Business Venturing* 22 (5): 613–27.

Gwartney, James, Robert Lawson, and Ryan Murphy. 2023. *Economic Freedom of the World: 2023 Annual Report*. Vancouver: The Fraser Institute.

Hayek, Friedrich A. von. 1945. "The Use of Knowledge in Society." *American Economic Review* 35 (4): 519–30.

Hébert, Robert F., and Albert N. Link. 1988. *The Entrepreneur: Mainstream Views and Radical Critiques*. New York: Praeger.

——— 1989. "In Search of the Meaning of Entrepreneurship." *Small Business Economics* 1 (1): 39–49. https://doi.org/10.1007/bf00389915.

——— 2009. *A History of Entrepreneurship*. London: Routledge.

Henrekson, Magnus, and Tino Sanandaji. 2011. "The Interaction of Entrepreneurship and Institutions." *Journal of Institutional Economics* 7 (1): 47–75.

Henrekson, Magnus, Christian Sandström, and Mikael Stenkula. 2024. *Moonshots and the New Industrial Policy: Questioning the Mission Economy*. Cham: Springer Nature.

Higgs, Robert. 1997. "Regime Uncertainty: Why the Great Depression Lasted So Long and Why Prosperity Resumed after the War." *The Independent Review* 1 (4): 561–90.

Hodgson, Geoffrey M. 2019. *Evolutionary Economics: Its Nature and Future*. Cambridge: Cambridge University Press.

Hoff, Trygve J. B. 1981. *Economic Calculation in the Socialist Society*. Translated by M. A. Michael. Indianapolis: Liberty Press.

Holcombe, Randall G. 2007. *Entrepreneurship and Economic Progress*. London: Routledge.

——— 2018. *Political Capitalism: How Political Influence Is Made and Maintained*. Cambridge: Cambridge University Press.

Huerta De Soto, Jesús. 2008. *The Theory of Dynamic Efficiency*. London: Routledge.

2009. *Money, Bank Credit, and Economic Cycles*. Auburn: Ludwig von Mises Institute.

Hutt, William H. 1939. *The Theory of Idle Resources*. Auburn: J. Cape.

Jevons, Willam Stanley. 1905. *The Principles of Economics: A Fragment of a Treatise on the Industrial Mechanism of Society and Other Papers*. New York: MacMillan.

Jones, Ronald W. 1965. "The Structure of Simple General Equilibrium Models." *Journal of Political Economy* 73 (6): 557–72.

Kim, Anthony B. 2023. *2024 Index of Economic Freedom*. Washington, DC: Heritage Foundation.

Kirzner, Israel M. 1973. *Competition and Entrepreneurship*. Chicago, IL: University of Chicago Press.

——— 1978. "Economics and Error." In *New Directions in Austrian Economics*, edited by Louis M. Spadaro, 57–76. Kansas City, MO: Sheed Andrews and McMeel.

——— 1997. *How Markets Work: Disequilibrium, Entrepreneurship and Discovery*. London: Institute of Economic Affairs.

Klein, Peter G. 2008. "Opportunity Discovery, Entrepreneurial Action, and Economic Organization." *Strategic Entrepreneurship Journal* 2 (3): 175–90.

Knight, Frank H. 1921. *Risk, Uncertainty and Profit*. New York: Houghton Mifflin.

Koellinger, Philipp. 2008. "Why Are Some Entrepreneurs More Innovative Than Others?" *Small Business Economics* 31: 21–37.

Koppl, Roger. 2018. *Expert Failure*. Cambridge: Cambridge University Press.

Koppl, Roger, Roberto Cazzolla Gatti, Abigail Devereaux et al. 2023. *Explaining Technology*. Cambridge: Cambridge University Press.

Lachmann, Ludwig M. 1943. "The Role of Expectations in Economics as a Social Science." *Economica* 10 (37): 12–23.

——— 1945. "A Note on the Elasticity of Expectations." *Economica* 12 (48): 248–53.

——— 1976. "From Mises to Shackle: An Essay on Austrian Economics and the Kaleidic Society." *Journal of Economic Literature* 14 (1): 54–62.

——— 1982. "Why Expectations Matter." *Investment Analysts Journal* 11 (20): 9–13.

Lazear, Edward P. 2004. "Balanced Skills and Entrepreneurship." *American Economic Review* 94 (2): 208–11.

Lerner, Josh. 2009. *Boulevard of Broken Dreams*. Princeton: Princeton University Press.

Levine, Ross, and Yona Rubinstein. 2017. "Smart and Illicit: Who Becomes an Entrepreneur and Do They Earn More?" *The Quarterly Journal of Economics* 132 (2): 963–1018.

Malerba, Franco, and Maureen McKelvey. 2019. "Knowledge-Intensive Innovative Entrepreneurship." *Foundations and Trends® in Entrepreneurship* 14 (6): 555–681.

——— 2020. "Knowledge-Intensive Innovative Entrepreneurship Integrating Schumpeter, Evolutionary Economics, and Innovation Systems." *Small Business Economics* 54 (2): 503–22.

Mazzucato, Mariana. 2011. *The Entrepreneurial State*. London: Demos.

——— 2018. "Mission-Oriented Innovation Policies: Challenges and Opportunities." *Industrial and Corporate Change* 27 (5): 803–15.

McCaffrey, Matthew. 2016. "Good Judgment, Good Luck: Frank Fetter's Neglected Theory of Entrepreneurship." *Review of Political Economy* 28 (4): 504–22.

McCaffrey, Matthew, and Joseph T. Salerno. 2011. "A Theory of Political Entrepreneurship." *Modern Economy* 2 (4): 552–60.

McCraw, Thomas K. 2007. *Prophet of Innovation: Joseph Schumpeter and Creative Destruction*. Harvard, MA: Harvard University Press.

McKelvie, Alexander, J. Michael Haynie, and Veronica Gustavsson. 2011. "Unpacking the Uncertainty Construct: Implications for Entrepreneurial Action." *Journal of Business Venturing* 26 (3): 273–92.

McMullen, Jeffery S. 2015. "Entrepreneurial Judgment as Empathic Accuracy: A Sequential Decision-Making Approach to Entrepreneurial Action." *Journal of Institutional Economics* 11 (3): 651–81.

McMullen, Jeffery S., and Dean A. Shepherd. 2006. "Entrepreneurial Action and the Role of Uncertainty in the Theory of the Entrepreneur." *Academy of Management Review* 31 (1): 132–52.

Menger, Carl. 2007. *Principles of Economics*. Translated by James Dingwall and Bert F. Hoselitz. Auburn, AL: Ludwig von Mises Institute.

Metcalfe, J. Stanley. 2002. *Evolutionary Economics and Creative Destruction*. London: Routledge.

Mingardi, Alberto. 2015. "A Critique of Mazzucato's Entrepreneurial State." *Cato Journal* 35 (3): 603–25.

Mises, Ludwig von. 1935. "Economic Calculation in the Socialist Commonwealth." In *Collectivist Economic Planning*, edited by F. A. Hayek, 87–130. London: George Routledge & Sons.

——— 1951. *Socialism: An Economic and Sociological Analysis*. Translated by J. Kahane. New Haven, CT: Yale University Press.

——— 1953. *The Theory of Money and Credit*. New Haven, CT: Yale University Press.

——— 1998. *Human Action: A Treatise on Economics*. The Scholar's Edition. Auburn, AL: Ludwig von Mises Institute.

2008. "Profit and Loss." In *Planning for Freedom: Let the Market System Work*, edited by Bettina Bien Greaves, 143–72. Indianapolis, IN: Liberty Fund.

Nelson, Richard R. 1995. "Recent Evolutionary Theorizing about Economic Change." *Journal of Economic Literature* 33 (1): 48–90.

2005. "14 Perspectives on Technological Evolution." In *The Evolutionary Foundations of Economics*, edited by Kurt Dopfer, 461–71. Cambridge: Cambridge University Press.

2018. "Economics from an Evolutionary Perspective." In *Modern Evolutionary Economics: An Overview*, edited by Richard R. Nelson, Giovanni Dosi, Constance E., Helfat et al., 1–34. Cambridge: Cambridge University Press.

Nelson, Richard R., and Sidney G. Winter. 1973. "Toward an Evolutionary Theory of Economic Capabilities." *The American Economic Review* 63 (2): 440–49.

1974. "Neoclassical vs. Evolutionary Theories of Economic Growth: Critique and Prospectus." *The Economic Journal* 84 (336): 886–905.

1982. *An Evolutionary Theory of Economic Change*. Cambridge, MA: The Belknap Press of Harvard University Press.

North, Douglass C. 1990. *Institutions, Institutional Change and Economic Performance*. Cambridge: Cambridge University Press.

1991. "Institutions." *Journal of Economic Perspectives* 5 (1): 97–112.

1994. "Economic Performance through Time." *American Economic Review* 84 (3): 359–68.

Packard, Mark D., and Per L. Bylund. 2021. "From Homo Economicus to Homo Agens: Toward a Subjective Rationality for Entrepreneurship." *Journal of Business Venturing* 36 (6): 106159. https://doi.org/10.1016/j.jbusvent.2021.106159.

forthcoming. "Towards an Entrepreneurial Judgement Theory: Building the Cognitive Microfoundations of Entrepreneurial Judgement." *International Small Business Journal*.

Packard, Mark D., Brent B. Clark, and Peter G. Klein. 2017. "Uncertainty Types and Transitions in the Entrepreneurial Process." *Organization Science* 28 (5): 840–56.

Parker, Simon C. 2004. *The Economics of Self-Employment and Entrepreneurship*. Cambridge: Cambridge University Press.

Potts, Jason, and Kurt Dopfer. 2024. "New Evolutionary Economics." https://ssrn.com/abstract=4837360.

Rothbard, Murray N. 2000. *America's Great Depression*. 5th ed. Auburn, AL: Ludwig von Mises Institute.

2004. *Man, Economy, and State with Power and Market. Scholar's Edition*. Auburn, AL: Ludwig von Mises Institute.

Sachs, Jeffrey D., and Andrew M. Warner. 1999. "The Big Rush, Natural Resource Booms and Growth." *Journal of Development Economics* 59 (1): 43–76.

Salerno, Joseph T. 2008. "The Entrepreneur: Real and Imagined." *Quarterly Journal of Austrian Economics* 11 (3): 188–207.

——— 2012. "A Reformulation of Austrian Business Cycle Theory in Light of the Financial Crisis." *Quarterly Journal of Austrian Economics* 15 (1): 3–44.

Sautet, Frederic E. 2013. "Local and Systemic Entrepreneurship: Solving the Puzzle of Entrepreneurship and Economic Development." *Entrepreneurship Theory and Practice* 37 (2): 387–402.

Say, Jean Baptiste. 1836. *A Treatise on Political Economy: Or the Production, Distribution, and Consumption of Wealth*. Philadelphia: Grigg & Elliot.

Schumpeter, Joseph A. 1909. "On the Concept of Social Value." *The Quarterly Journal of Economics* 23 (2): 213–32.

——— 1934. *The Theory of Economic Development: An Inquiry into Profits, Capital, Credit, Interest, and the Business Cycle*. Cambridge, MA: Harvard University Press.

——— 1947. *Capitalism, Socialism, and Democracy*. 2nd ed. New York: Harper & Bros.

Shackle, G. L. S. 1979. *Imagination and the Nature of Choice*. Edinburgh: Edinburgh University Press.

Shane, Scott. 2003. *A General Theory of Entrepreneurship: The Individual-Opportunity Nexus*. Cheltenham: Edward Elgar.

Smith, Adam. 1976. *An Inquiry into the Nature and Causes of the Wealth of Nations*. Chicago, IL: University of Chicago Press.

Sobel, Russell S. 2008. "Testing Baumol: Institutional Quality and the Productivity of Entrepreneurship." *Journal of Business Venturing* 23 (6): 641–55.

Stigler, George J. 1957. "Perfect Competition, Historically Contemplated." *Journal of Political Economy* 65 (1): 1–17.

Thornton, Mark. 1998. "Richard Cantillon and the Origin of Economic Theory." *Journal Des Économistes et Des Études Humaines* 8 (1): 61–74.

——— 2020. "Turning the Word Upside down: How Cantillon Redefined the Entrepreneur." *Quarterly Journal of Austrian Economics* 23 (3–4): 265–80.

Venkataraman, Sankaran. 1997. "The Distinctive Domain of Entrepreneurship Research. J. Katz, R. Brockhaus, Eds." *Advances in Entrepreneurship, Firm Emergence and Growth* 3: 119–38.

Webb, Justin W., Laszlo Tihanyi, R. Duane Ireland, and David G. Sirmon. 2009. "You Say Illegal, I Say Legitimate: Entrepreneurship in the Informal Economy." *Academy of Management Review* 34 (3): 492–510.

Wennberg, Karl, and Christian Sandström. 2022. *Questioning the Entrepreneurial State: Status-Quo, Pitfalls, and the Need for Credible Innovation Policy*. Cham: Springer Nature.

Wennekers, Sander, and Roy Thurik. 1999. "Linking Entrepreneurship and Economic Growth." *Small Business Economics* 13 (1): 27–56. https://doi.org/10.1023/a:1008063200484.

Wicksell, Knut. 1936. *Interest and Prices: A Study of the Causes Regulating the Value of Money*. New York: Sentry Press.

Williamson, Oliver E. 2000. "The New Institutional Economics: Taking Stock, Looking Ahead." *Journal of Economic Literature* 38 (3): 595–613.

Winter, Sidney G. 2006. "Toward a Neo-Schumpeterian Theory of the Firm." *Industrial and Corporate Change* 15 (1): 125–41.

Witt, Ulrich. 1994. "Evolutionary Economics." In *The Elgar Companion to Austrian Economics*, edited by Peter J. Boettke, 541–48. Cheltenham: Edward Elgar.

———. 2006. "Evolutionary Economics." 0605. Papers on Economics and Evolution. Jena: Max Planck Institute of Economics. www.econstor.eu/bitstream/10419/31834/1/518416216.pdf.

Wood, Matthew S., Per Bylund, and Steven Bradley. 2016. "The Influence of Tax and Regulatory Policies on Entrepreneurs' Opportunity Evaluation Decisions." *Management Decision* 54 (5): 1160–82.

Acknowledgments

The author has benefited from comments and suggestions on previous drafts from Fernando D'Andrea, Hunter Hastings, David Myeongho Park, and Jason Potts. Feedback from Jesper Bylund, Susanne Bylund, Chandra Dubey, Mark Packard, Ryan Turnipseed, and Cazzie Williams is also gratefully acknowledged. The scholarly camaraderie and overall supportive atmosphere at Universidad Rey Juan Carlos in Madrid during spring semester 2024 also helped, as did comments from two anonymous reviewers. The usual caveat applies: any and all remaining errors, mistakes, and blunders are the author's. Financial support from Oklahoma State University and the Institute for Humane Studies helped make this project possible.

Cambridge Elements =

Evolutionary Economics

John Foster
University of Queensland

John Foster is Emeritus Professor of Economics and former Head of the School of Economics at the University of Queensland, Brisbane. He is Fellow of the Academy of Social Science in Australia, Life member of Clare Hall College, Cambridge and Past President of the International J.A. Schumpeter Society.

Jason Potts
RMIT University

Jason Potts is Professor of Economics at RMIT University, Melbourne. He is also an Adjunct Fellow at the Institute of Public Affairs. His research interests include technological change, economics of innovation, and economics of cities. He was the winner of the 2000 International Joseph A. Schumpeter Prize and has published over 60 articles and six books.

Isabel Almudi
University of Zaragoza

Isabel Almudi is Professor of Economics at the University of Zaragoza, Spain, where she also belongs to the Instituto de Biocomputación y Física de Sistemas Complejos. She has been Visiting Fellow at the European University Institute, Columbia University and RMIT University. Her research fields are evolutionary economics, innovation studies, environmental economics and dynamic systems.

Francisco Fatas-Villafranca
University of Zaragoza

Francisco Fatas-Villafranca is Professor of Economics at the University of Zaragoza, Spain. He has been Visiting Scholar at Columbia University and Visiting Researcher at the University of Manchester. His research focuses on economic theory and quantitative methods in the social sciences, with special interest in evolutionary economics.

David A. Harper
New York University

David A. Harper is Clinical Professor of Economics and Co-Director of the Program on the Foundations of the Market Economy at New York University. His research interests span institutional economics, Austrian economics and evolutionary economics. He has written two books and has published extensively in academic journals. He was formerly Chief Analyst and Manager at the New Zealand Treasury.

About the Series

Cambridge Elements of Evolutionary Economics provides authoritative and up-to-date reviews of core topics and recent developments in the field. It includes state-of-the-art contributions on all areas in the field. The series is broadly concerned with questions of dynamics and change, with a particular focus on processes of entrepreneurship and innovation, industrial and institutional dynamics, and on patterns of economic growth and development.

Cambridge Elements⁼

Evolutionary Economics

Elements in the Series

A Reconsideration of the Theory of Non-Linear Scale Effects: The Sources of Varying Returns to, and Economics of, Scale
Richard G. Lipsey

Evolutionary Economics: Its Nature and Future
Geoffrey M. Hodgson

Coevolution in Economic Systems
Isabel Almudi and Francisco Fatas-Villafranca

Industrial Policy: The Coevolution of Public and Private Sources of Finance for Important Emerging and Evolving Technologies
Kenneth I. Carlaw and Richard G. Lipsey

Explaining Technology
Roger Koppl, Roberto Cazzolla Gatti, Abigail Devereaux, Brian D. Fath, James Herriot, Wim Hordijk, Stuart Kauffman, Robert E. Ulanowicz and Sergi Valverde

Evolutionary Games and the Replicator Dynamics
Saul Mendoza-Palacios and Onésimo Hernández-Lerma

The Dynamic Metacapabilities Framework: Introducing Quantum Management and the Informational View of the Firm
Harold Paredes-Frigolett and Andreas Pyka

Entrepreneurship and Evolutionary Economics
Per L. Bylund

A full series listing is available at: www.cambridge.org/EEVE

For EU product safety concerns, contact us at Calle de José Abascal, 56–1°, 28003 Madrid, Spain or eugpsr@cambridge.org.

www.ingramcontent.com/pod-product-compliance
Lightning Source LLC
LaVergne TN
LVHW020352260326
834688LV00045B/1680